A JOHN CATT PUBLICATION

Kate Jones

WILIAM & L

FIVE FORMATIVE ASSESSMENT STRATEGIES
IN ACTION

IN ACTION SERIES

EDITOR
TOM SHERRINGTON

FOREWORD BY JOHN HATTIE
COVER ILLUSTRATION BY OLIVER CAVIGLIOLI

A
WALKTHRUs
PRODUCTION

First Published 2021

by John Catt Educational Ltd,
15 Riduna Park, Station Road,
Melton, Woodbridge IP12 1QT

Tel: +44 (0) 1394 389850
Email: enquiries@johncatt.com
Website: www.johncatt.com

ISBN: 978 1 913622 77 0

Set and designed by John Catt Educational Limited

SERIES FOREWORD

TOM SHERRINGTON

The idea for the *In Action* series was developed by John Catt's *Teaching WalkThrus* team after we saw how popular our *Rosenshine's Principles in Action* booklets proved to be. We realised that the same approach might support teachers to access the ideas of a range of researchers, cognitive scientists and educators. A constant challenge that we wrestle with in the world of teaching and education research is the significant distance between the formulation of a set of concepts and conclusions that might be useful to teachers and the moment when a teacher uses those ideas to teach their students in a more effective manner, thereby succeeding in securing deeper or richer learning. Sometimes so much meaning is lost along that journey, through all the communication barriers that line the road, that the implementation of the idea bears no relation to the concept its originator had in mind. Sometimes it's more powerful to hear from a teacher about how they implemented an idea than it is to read about the idea from a researcher or cognitive scientist directly – because they reduce that distance; they push some of those barriers aside.

In our *In Action* series, the authors and their collaborative partners are all teachers or school leaders close to the action in classrooms in real schools. Their strategies for translating their subjects' work into practice bring fresh energy to a powerful set of original ideas in a way that we're confident will support teachers with their professional learning and, ultimately, their classroom practice. In doing so, they are also paying their respects to the original researchers and their work. In education, as in so many walks of life, we are standing on the shoulders of giants. We believe that our selection of featured researchers and papers represents some of the most important work done in the field of education in recent times.

This *In Action* book is an excellent addition to the series, bringing together a powerful set of research-informed ideas and a superb teacher-communicator. Dylan Wiliam's work on formative assessment has been hugely influential across the education sector for over 25 years, sharpening our understanding of the concepts, highlighting the nature of effective feedback and the role of responsive teaching in the classroom. The 'five strategies', formulated with

3

Siobhán Leahy, represent one of the most powerful frameworks for thinking about teaching that we have. Kate Jones was an obvious choice to ask to take this book on. Her series of books on retrieval practice has been a massive success, showcasing her considerable skill as a communicator of ideas – blending an authentic enthusiasm for teaching, a deep engagement with the research and the pragmatism that only arises from spending many years in the classroom, delivering the goods!

As Kate explains in her introduction, this book will support teachers who have already engaged with Wiliam and Leahy's publications as well as anyone who has yet to read their work directly. Each chapter focuses on one of the five strategies, providing a rich array of practical ideas for teachers to implement in their classrooms. Finally, huge thanks to John Hattie for writing an excellent foreword for the book. He captures the spirit of the whole endeavour brilliantly, as well as making the Welsh connection that Dylan and Kate share.

FOREWORD

BY JOHN HATTIE

We all owe a great debt to Wales. The Welsh have provided us with the equal sign, ball bearings, the microphone, mail-order shopping, the spare wheel, the breathalyser, the second-longest town name (Llanfairpwllgwyngyllgogerychwyrndrobwllllantysiliogogogoch, the first being in New Zealand: Taumatawhakatangihangakoauauotamateaturipuka kapikimaungahoronukupokaiwhenuakitanatahu), great rugby teams, Dylan Wiliam, and Kate Jones.

I recall the time when I first appreciated the power of Dylan's work; I was asked to write a commentary of his work as part of a special issue of the journal where 'the black box' research was first published. My commentary slipped into a footnote, barely mentioned, but his work along with Siobhán Leahy, Paul Black, and now many others, has changed our landscape, our ways of seeing the world, and impacted the lives of so many teachers and students. Kate Jones has done Dylan and Siobhán an honour in writing this book which makes their core notions even more accessible to a new generation.

While Dylan and I disagree on many matters (e.g., the role of meta-analysis), our conclusions are remarkably similar – not surprising as we read, research, and critique on similar evidence bases, both work in classrooms to see and learn from the impact of ideas, and surround ourselves with the world's best critics that helps enhance our work. Siobhán Leahy has written much on implementing these ideas, and Kate Jones just 'loves to teach'. This book is focused on five powerful ideas, puts the focus on the impact of teaching on the learning lives of students, and asks teachers to become evaluators of their impact. The three questions that lead to these ideas are firmly learner-oriented. Where is the learning going? Where is the learner now? And, how does the learner get there? These three questions build on the resources a student brings to the class, respects the student by understanding their current learning, and uses this understanding to move forward. The five ideas beg for teachers to have high levels of clarity, to choose tasks that elicit evidence of learning and progress, to provide feedback that moves learning forward, to encourage students to collectively impact on each other, and to see students as owners of their own learning.

Note, the word 'assessment' is not used (yet), but becomes a means to understand, enact, and deliver on these big five. Note, the focus is forward-looking whereas most classes work in the 'present' – do and complete this work, do activities, and move with the bell on to the next set of activities. Lots of doing and, for too many students, not enough acknowledging what they already know or showing them that where this learning is leading them. Note, the high levels of expertise needed by teachers to interpret evidence of learning or not learning, requiring what can be termed as 'evaluative thinking' (Rickards et al, 2021). Note, it is very much the student who needs to be taught this evaluative thinking about their assessments. Too many assessments stop with the number, indicating that that work is over, with little attempt to evaluate the results for students and teachers to then optimally move forward.

It is great to see these five ideas anchor the book and not formative assessment. As Jones noted, formative assessment has the potential to be misunderstood, and it is sad that the word 'assessment' is even in the phrase as it turns most minds to testing and forgets the fundamental meaning of 'formative'. If only the term had been 'formative evaluation', placing more emphasis on the interpretations that allow moving forward. It was changed from evaluation to assessment by Bloom (et al, 1971), although he still called his book *The Handbook of Formative and Summative Evaluation*. The striving ahead based on interpretive evidence is all summed up in their earlier definition of formative practice: 'Practice in a classroom is formative to the extent that evidence about student achievement is elicited, interpreted, and used by teachers, learners, or their peers, to make decisions about the next steps in instruction that are likely to be better, or better founded, than the decisions they would have taken in the absence of the evidence that was elicited.' (Black and Wiliam, 2009, p. 9)

Students often are asked to all get on the bus, being driven by the teacher somewhere but not necessarily knowing where to, and then being asked to get off at the end of the lesson. No wonder schooling can be of little enjoyment and seen as random encounters with activities but unclear where it is all leading. Wiliam (2009) commented that if students know where they are headed, then they have more chance of arriving at the destination. Schooling should be more like getting in an Uber – the destination clear from the outset and then the focus on moving from where they are now to where they need to be, with multiple ways and times to get there. Often, we need to know we are on the right track, sometimes we need to stop for a coffee or McDonalds and it is okay if we go off track as GPS can resolve this (without telling us we are dummies), and we can sightsee on the way if we wish. But it all depends on knowing the destination.

Jones describes many of the misunderstandings of learning intentions and success criteria. A clear message is that teachers need to hear how students are understanding the intentions and success of the lesson. It is not enough to proclaim them, put them on the wall or smartboard, but to hear how the students are understanding what it means to be successful as they need to be the drivers towards their destination. We have found that – despite magnificent teacher success criteria – too often, students still see learning as knowing lots, emulating Siri and Alexa, and just getting the work done (no matter the quality). The clarity of knowing where you are going sensitises students to the value of assessment, feedback, peer reactions, and getting there evokes emotions of joy and fun in learning.

Then to 'hear' students' thinking, the desirable struggles, the stops and starts are why classroom discussion is so important. It is so obvious, so why is it so absent so often? The dominant talker too often is the teacher, and the majority of their questions require three-word answers usually focused on facts. No, says Jones citing Wiliam and Leahy's (2015) research, questions should cause thinking and propel students forward. Teachers may need to rethink themselves as model listeners, listening to how students are thinking, listening to student questions, hear where they may go off-road, and listen as students hear, understand and action feedback. Surely listening is one of the best ways to show respect for students? The insight is that unless students hear, understand, and action feedback, it is unlikely to improve their learning.

As Nuthall (2007) noted, most feedback students receive about their work comes from other students, and too often it is incorrect feedback that can hinder progress and engagement in the learning. Wiliam and Leahy (2015) address this directly, claiming that we need to activate students as learning resources for one another. Our recent work has focused on the skills and confidence to contribute to others and how this requires deliberate teaching and not merely putting students in groups, hoping and wishing they can teach and learn from each other. They note the importance of group goals and accountability, and we argue that it should be both individual and group goals, tasks, and accountability. What is the contribution each student is making to their own and to the group, does the task require multiple interpretations, and are students accountable for their own as well as contributions to the group performance? As noted in this book, employers are now asking for team players and students need to be taught the skills and develop the confidence to contribute to group tasks. They need to appreciate they are all 'in the same boat', can teach and learn from each other, and can arrive at the destination faster and more effectively together than alone.

All major ideas in this book lead to one major finding: students need to be deliberately taught to regulate their own learning, and so self-regulation dominates on most pages. When students learn to become their own teachers, they are less and less reliant on us. Teachers need to learn to gradually release responsibility, to slow the teaching to enhance the speed of learning, and when 'students are owners of their own learning, all the other strategies fall into place' (Wiliam and Leahy, 2015). This, claims Jones, is 'the holy grail of teaching and learning' (although Monty Python nor I ever found this grail).

It is a gift to have a translator to mobilise powerful research, and this book is an illustration of the high standards that we associate with the work of Wiliam, Leahy, and Jones. Enjoy.

John Hattie, Emeritus Laureate Professor at Melbourne Graduate School of Education, Chair of the Board of the Australian Institute for Teaching and School Leadership, and author of *Visible Learning*

ACKNOWLEDGEMENTS

When I was asked by Tom Sherrington and John Catt to write this book, I immediately jumped at the chance to do so for a variety of reasons. Although Dylan Wiliam is known as a world-leading expert in the field of education, I naturally felt a strong Welsh connection as we are both very proud to be from Wales. I have learned a huge amount from Dylan and Siobhán Leahy, especially with formative assessment. The chance to revisit and reflect on their work, delve deeper and share how I have implemented and embedded formative assessment strategies in action in my classroom was an opportunity not to be missed!

The *In Action* series is proving to be incredibly popular amongst classroom teachers and school leaders. I can recall reading *Rosenshine's Principles In Action* and being blown away by the powerful simplicity of the book. It's informative, practical and has become a book I refer to again and again. It is a wonderful exploration and discussion of a seminal piece of work by Barak Rosenshine. Writing this book, which is considerably shorter than my previous books, I have discovered how difficult it is to explain key concepts, research and ideas in short chapters. It is a real skill that I did not recognise until this process – that was our aim, to keep the book clear, concise and helpful. To be published alongside other authors as part of the *In Action* series is a real privilege. I always enjoy working with Tom Sherrington, the series editor, as I am continually learning from him and he is always very supportive and encouraging.

Thanks to all the teachers and leaders that have contributed case studies to this book. Although I am a classroom teacher and leader, it was essential to include examples outside of my own subject and cover a range of ages taught. The case studies highlight how teachers are using formative assessment strategies across a range of subjects and phases.

Another thank you must go to the wonderful Professor John Hattie for writing the foreword. Throughout my career, I have read and followed his work, as have so many teachers and school leaders around the world. Hattie's work has had a direct impact on my classroom practice. A well-known message that he promotes is 'know thy impact' and formative assessment can – and should – have a positive impact on teaching and learning.

Finally, from the beginning, Dylan Wiliam has played a very important role in the process of writing this book. I have sent him chapters, which he has carefully read and provided lots of valuable insight, thorough feedback and guidance. The input from Dylan has enhanced this book significantly. The opportunity to work with him has been the professional highlight of my career thus far and I feel incredibly lucky. Dylan – *diolch yn fawr iawn*.

TABLE OF CONTENTS

INTRODUCTION

Dylan Wiliam and Siobhán Leahy's *Embedding Formative Assessment* has been incredibly influential and impactful in schools around the world. Wiliam and Leahy are able to expertly communicate academic research to teachers whilst also providing a plethora of classroom examples to illustrate how the research can effectively be applied in a classroom context. This approach has greatly supported me as a classroom teacher and middle leader.

What is formative assessment?

There has been a lot written about the definition of formative assessment. Wiliam has explored this question as there are various interpretations from different authors and educators. Wiliam and Paul Black (1998) originally defined formative assessment as: 'encompassing all those activities undertaken by teachers, and/or their students, which provide information to be used as feedback to modify the teaching and learning activities in which they are engaged.'

Formative assessment is essentially a range of evidence-informed strategies that teachers can use to support their learners to make progress. Wiliam and Leahy (2015) write about five key strategies that can support the effective implementation of formative assessment, building on the work of other leading educators and academics, and that has been the inspiration and focus of this book. Formative assessment can help both the teacher and student understand what needs to be learned and how this can be achieved. Also, during the learning process, formative assessment can identify students' progress as well as highlighting gaps in their knowledge and understanding to give the teacher useful insight as to what feedback and instruction can be provided to continue to move learners forward.

Formative assessment takes place during the learning process. It continually informs the teacher and student as to how learning can move forward as it is happening. This is different to summative assessment, which focuses on evaluation of student learning at the end of the process, for example, an end of topic test that is not used as a low stakes strategy but perhaps used for more formal recording and reporting.

The table below is a summary of the key components of *Embedding Formative Assessment*. The three key aspects are:

- Where the learner is going
- Where the learner is now
- How to get there

The table also illustrates the role and importance of the teacher, learner and peer in the formative assessment process.

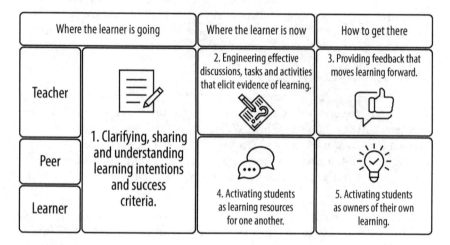

	Where the learner is going		Where the learner is now	How to get there
Teacher		1. Clarifying, sharing and understanding learning intentions and success criteria.	2. Engineering effective discussions, tasks and activities that elicit evidence of learning.	3. Providing feedback that moves learning forward.
Peer			4. Activating students as learning resources for one another.	5. Activating students as owners of their own learning.
Learner				

Do readers need to read *Embedding Formative Assessment*?

Despite the popularity of *Embedding Formative Assessment* and the fact it has been so widely referenced, I have not assumed that readers have read it while writing this book. This *In Action* book, in common with others in the series, aims to take the golden nuggets from the original text and show how they can be applied in the classroom. Although I would strongly recommend reading *Embedding Formative Assessment*, it is not essential in terms of being able to access and understand the ideas presented throughout this book.

Who is this book for?

This book was written for the classroom teacher, primary or secondary, to support their day-to-day practice. I have included a range of practical examples and case studies from different key stages and subjects as formative assessment applies to all teaching and learning from Early Years Foundation Stage to examination classes.

I also hope leaders at all levels will consider implementing, embedding or reflecting on how the formative assessment strategies are used in phases/ departments or across the whole school. Wiliam and Leahy often encourage teachers to collaborate with others, from writing learning intentions to planning higher order thinking questions. This is a message I have tried to stress too. I encourage teachers to collaborate with those in and outside of their schools, either in phase or subject communities or via social media channels such as Facebook and/or Twitter.

What do I hope teachers and leaders will take away from this book?

The book is structured so that each of the five chapters is based on a strand of formative assessment. The chapters can be read in isolation or all in one sitting. I hope it is a book that teachers and leaders will return to repeatedly as they continually review and reflect on their practice. There are practical examples that can be implemented into classroom practice, as well as plentiful words of advice from Wiliam and Leahy, and a range of case studies from other classroom practitioners and leaders. Formative assessment, as with a lot of concepts and approaches in education, has the potential to be misunderstood and – what has been described by Ed Haertel (Brown and Campione, 1996) – 'lethally mutated' into something far removed from what it originally intended to be. I hope this book can address any misconceptions surrounding formative assessment and instead illustrate how important all of these key strategies are to effective teaching and learning.

CHAPTER 1

CLARIFYING, SHARING AND UNDERSTANDING LEARNING INTENTIONS AND SUCCESS CRITERIA

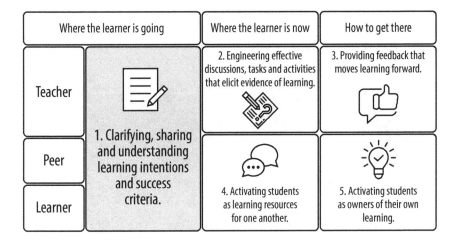

	Where the learner is going	Where the learner is now	How to get there
Teacher	1. Clarifying, sharing and understanding learning intentions and success criteria.	2. Engineering effective discussions, tasks and activities that elicit evidence of learning.	3. Providing feedback that moves learning forward.
Peer		4. Activating students as learning resources for one another.	5. Activating students as owners of their own learning.
Learner			

What do Wiliam and Leahy say about learning intentions and success criteria?

- 'Before we can find out what our learners are learning, before we can give feedback, before we can engage our learners as resources for one another and as owners of their own learning, we have to be clear about where we are going.'

- 'It is, in general, a good idea that students know where they are going – we are both embarrassed about how long we spent teaching without telling our students where we were going. After all, it is really rather obvious that if our students know where we are headed, we are more likely to arrive at the correct destination.'

- 'We use learning intentions to describe the things that we want our students to learn and success criteria to describe the criteria that we use to judge whether the learning activities in which we engaged our students were successful.' (Wiliam and Leahy, 2015)

The work of Wiliam and Leahy makes clear that learning intentions and success criteria play an essential role in the learning journey for students. They should be an integral part of curriculum design and lesson planning and delivery. In addition to their importance for teachers and leaders, they serve an essential purpose in helping the students in our classes understand what they will be learning and how they can make progress. Wiliam has put it eloquently and simply that if students know where we are headed, then we have more chance of arriving at the destination (Learning Sciences International, 2018).

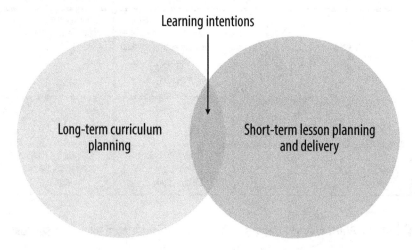

I recognise and understand the value of both learning intentions and success criteria but I have often struggled as to how this can actually be implemented and embedded effectively in lessons and across the overall curriculum. Using the ideas from Wiliam and Leahy, I have been able to gain greater clarity as to how learning intentions and success criteria can be effectively designed and communicated.

Through speaking to teachers about learning intentions, I have been surprised by the hostility and negative reaction. Clarifying, sharing and understanding learning intentions have been misunderstood in many schools. That is why this chapter is so important to identify and address common misconceptions.

Some schools are keen to share their model and approach but generally, as a profession, it's fair to say we haven't got this right... yet.

Before recommending some techniques and advice as to how learning intentions can be put into action in the classroom it might be useful to reflect on how this has been implemented and embedded in schools previously. Where have we gone wrong with learning intentions across schools and in lessons?

- Focusing on the lesson, not the learning
- Learning intentions shouldn't focus on activities and tasks
- Challenges and difficulties are not desirable
- Not using a clear language of learning
- Used to measure teacher performance
- Wasting precious lesson time

Fortunately, all of these negative aspects can easily be identified, addressed and rectified or prevented to ensure learning intentions are used effectively to support both teachers and students. Learning intentions can and should be helping, not hindering the learning process. Let's look at each one in turn.

Focus on the learning, not just a lesson

Wiliam and Leahy use the term 'learning intentions' as the most general possible term to describe any intentions the teacher has about what learners should learn, and thus can include objectives, goals, aims and so on. There is a distinction between learning and lessons. We know learning takes place over time, not restricted to one specific lesson. We should be focusing on planning the learning rather than planning singular lessons (although, of course, all teachers and leaders carry out both short and long-term planning). This is a fundamental and crucial difference to be aware of.

Author of *Boys Don't Try: Rethinking Masculinity in Schools*, Matt Pinkett has written about his frustration with lesson objectives. Pinkett (2017) writes, 'The idea that learning can be reduced to a single lesson target perpetuates the myth that learning is something that can be visible within the arbitrary units of time we call lessons.' A learning intention may span over one or more lessons. There is an element of flexibility with learning intentions and context is always key. We need to make a shift in terms of planning, mindset and delivery from lessons to long-term learning.

Focus on the content, skills and concepts that need to be learned, rather than the tasks and activities themselves

This is certainly something I have been guilty of in the past, focusing on what the students will be doing in a lesson rather than what they will be learning. This is where we see a flawed activity-led curriculum dominate and distract from the core knowledge, skills and concepts students need to learn. This is not to suggest that tasks and activities shouldn't be given careful consideration but they need to be selected and designed to support and enhance the learning and meet the learning intention.

Wiliam and Leahy have encountered this issue with a focus on tasks when talking to teachers about learning intentions. They write (2015, p. 27): 'When we ask teachers about their learning intentions for a particular lesson, it is common for them to reply by saying, "I'm going to have the students do this." In other words, teachers respond in terms of the activities in which they plan to engage their students. This is, of course, entirely understandable. The only way that teachers get students to learn is by engaging them in activities. However, if the teachers select activities without a clear view of the learning that is intended, it is far less likely that the students will learn what they need to learn. By engaging in an activity, students usually learn something, but not all outcomes of learning are equally valuable. By being clear about what it is we want students to learn—in Stephen Covey's words, by "starting with the end in mind" (Covey, 1989)—it is more likely that our students will learn what we need them to learn.' This is why we need to be mindful of the difference between what students will be learning and what students will be doing. Task design is important but should be an afterthought in terms of how it can aid the learning intention.

Challenges and difficulties are desirable

The work of Professors Elizabeth and Robert Bjork have highly influenced my practice and that of Wiliam too. They have written extensively about their research and the term they have coined, known as 'desirable difficulties' (2011). Desirable difficulties refer to the challenge that requires encoding and retrieval to support learning, comprehension and remembering. This is desirable in the classroom, but not *all* difficulties are desirable. If a student does not have the relevant background knowledge, understanding or skills to respond to a task or question successfully, the student will find the task difficult but is unlikely to learn anything from it.

As teachers, we need to ensure that the difficulties we present to our students are both accessible and desirable. In their popular book *Make It Stick: The*

Science of Successful Learning the authors Brown, Roediger and Mcdaniel (2014) state that for a task to be desirable the level of difficulty must be something that learners can overcome through increased effort. If students feel that achieving a goal is unlikely or unrealistic, then they will give up and this is undesirable. This level of desirable challenge should be central to all learning intentions.

A few years ago there became a trend of using some/most/all or must/should/could – differentiated lesson objectives. They continue to be used in schools although not as widely used and promoted as previously. Teacher and senior leader Rachel Ball has written on her popular blog (The Educational Imposters, 2020) that, 'By having differentiated learning objectives or outcomes we are instantly saying that not all the work is achievable for all.' This can suggest we have lower expectations for some learners in our classes. This is clearly not a message we should be promoting and instead encourage desirable difficulties in the classroom.

Wiliam and Leahy (2015) are very clear to state that learning intentions should be the same for the whole group, but success criteria may be differentiated. Below is an example of some/most/all lesson objectives:

- *All* will be able to *describe* the different reasons why Henry VIII broke with Rome.

- *Most* will be able to *explain* the different reasons why Henry VIII broke with Rome.

- *Some* will be able to *evaluate* the different reasons why Henry VIII broke with the Roman Catholic Church.

This can be changed and rephrased to provide a desirable level of difficulty for all learners in the classroom, as shown below:

Learning intention: To explore the different reasons why Henry VIII broke with the Roman Catholic Church and understand the significance of each factor.

This learning intention could lead to an interesting discussion about two key skills in the study of history, causation and significance. Alternatively, this could simply be an enquiry key or big question, as we will discover. This is not differentiated but the success criteria can be to provide the necessary support and challenge for all learners in the classroom. Teachers can provide differentiation by having the same question for all students, but providing different levels of support or challenge.

Big question: Why did Henry VIII break with the Roman Catholic Church?

Use a clear language of learning

I have encountered learning intentions that are very complex in terms of the language used. I think that has been partly a result of teachers using examination specifications and assessment objective mark schemes to write learning intentions. Specifications and mark schemes are written for teachers and can become lost in translation when trying to share with students if not explained with precise clarity. The role of the teacher is to articulate the learning intentions well, either in writing and/or verbally – ideally, it is best to do both.

There can also be the temptation to include too much information and content in a learning intention and this is where they can become over-complicated. They should purposefully be brief and give an overview. It can be challenging to condense this information, especially when we consider the different elements students will need to learn in terms of content, concepts, skills and vocabulary. It is important that teachers are mindful when including subject-specific vocabulary in learning intentions. Students need a secure grasp of the terminology included and must be able to retrieve the meaning in the correct context. It is usually worth revisiting key terms when explaining learning intentions and to be mindful of the curse of knowledge. Do not assume our students know, understand or can recall the vocabulary even if we have covered it in previous lessons.

In recent years, teachers have gained more insight into the concept of dual coding, where information can be communicated through two different formats to transfer through two different channels to the memory, for example combining words and images. The crucial aspect with dual coding is that it must not overload working memory, which is limited in terms of both duration (how long information can be held) and capacity (how much information can be held). Paul Chandler and John Sweller (1991) found that students learned less when a diagram of blood flow in the heart was accompanied by text, even when the text was integrated into the diagram to lessen what they refer to as the 'split attention' effect.

This can be applied to learning intentions and can be very useful to help students with English as an additional language (EAL) or to support learners with special educational needs and disabilities (SEND) to fully grasp and comprehend the set intentions. The selected images or icons must be thought about carefully and must be relevant as there is potential for them to be distracting and confusing, and too many icons can be overwhelming. The icons can promote meaningful and relevant discussion, as shown with the example below:

Learning intention: To understand the theme and significance of social class in the play *Blood Brothers*.

This specific example can be viewed as complex as students will need to grasp the concepts of themes within a play and also social class, either through recall if this has been previously covered or as part of the lesson to achieve the specific learning intention. This can also be made explicit in the success criteria.

Not used to measure teacher performance but instead understand the content of a lesson by an observer

An intense focus on learning intentions became linked to how good a teacher was. They were essential for graded lesson observations, became an inspection tick box and moved far away from what Wiliam and Leahy had originally written about. An observer should certainly understand and be aware of the learning intentions, not to judge the teacher but to gauge the understanding and progress that learners are making in the class.

We need to move away from an observer and teacher viewpoint, checking to see if the learning intention has been achieved at the end of the lesson because the reality is that learning takes place over time. How long it takes can be dependent on a range of factors. Learning intentions must be revisited at a later date to distinguish between student performance and learning. This has been a complete game-changer for me, and many others, in how I view and approach teaching and learning. This, once again, is based on the groundbreaking work of Bjork and Bjork (2011) who define performance and learning as:

Performance: what we can observe and measure during instruction or training.

Learning: a more or less permanent change in knowledge or understanding that is the target of instruction.

We need to allow some time for forgetting to pass, then later check if the learning intention has been achieved with recall from long-term memory in contrast to performance in the lesson.

Learning intentions can be time-efficient

Many teachers – myself included – have previously turned lesson objectives into novelty tasks where students had to guess what the objective was based on an activity or how an object was linked to the objective. There were occasions in my lessons where the learning intentions would be communicated to my class via emoji! We need to move away from the novelty and gimmickry. Creating anagrams or codes for students to solve the learning intention is well-intentioned in the sense of providing an engaging task or hook for learners but, ultimately, this is wasting valuable time. Asking students to solve or guess the learning intention can cause confusion where there should be clarity. Instead, starting lessons with regular retrieval practice tasks can be engaging, enjoyable and is ultimately a more effective and efficient use of time.

We know that just because students have copied down learning intentions, it does not mean they have understood them. Also, the most obvious issue is the time wasted. It is absurd to insist children mindlessly copy down lesson objectives. It's important to make clear that I do not think learning intentions are a waste of time – far from it – but students copying them down certainly is, and the same can be argued with success criteria. Time should be spent explaining and discussing the learning intentions to ensure all learners fully grasp them, hence the importance of clarifying, sharing and understanding.

Key questions I would pose to senior and middle leaders that are enforcing policies linked to learning intentions are the following (if these are happening at your school):

- Why do learning intentions need to be on display or visible at all times in a lesson?
- Is there an issue with just using verbal learning intentions? If so, what is the issue or concern?
- Why do students need to have learning intentions written down?
- How much time is given to staff to plan, design and reflect on learning intentions?
- How much time in lessons is expected to be spent on learning intentions?
- Is there consistency across departments and key stages with learning intentions and success criteria in lessons?

Tips for clarifying, sharing and understanding learning intentions

Wiliam and Leahy write, 'Developing good learning intentions is not easy and our work with teachers suggests that this first strategy may actually be the most difficult of the formative assessment strategies to implement well.' I agree, writing and designing effective learning intentions seems simple but is actually more complex than it appears. Below are some suggestions to consider when writing and implementing learning intentions across the curriculum.

Writing and designing learning intentions

Are the learning intentions explicitly clear for both the students and the teacher? Is everyone in the classroom on the same page in terms of understanding? When writing learning intentions and success criteria, whichever way they are presented, I suggest considering these three golden rules:

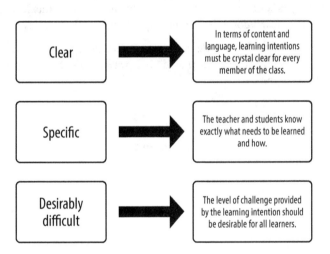

Clear → In terms of content and language, learning intentions must be crystal clear for every member of the class.

Specific → The teacher and students know exactly what needs to be learned and how.

Desirably difficult → The level of challenge provided by the learning intention should be desirable for all learners.

Examples in action in the classroom

Examples of learning intentions across a range of subjects and key stages that are clear, specific and desirably difficult.

Year 4 religious education class

Learning intention: To be able to identify and recognise artefacts of importance in Judaism.

Year 5 English grammar lesson

Learning intention: To adapt writing for different readers and different purposes by changing vocabulary, tone and sentence structure to suit the audience, e.g., simplifying for younger readers.

Year 10 English literature class

Learning intention: To comprehend Orwell's use of allegory and satire within the characterisation of *Animal Farm*.

Teacher and author of *Full on Learning: Involve Me and I'll Understand*, Zoe Elder suggests adding 'so that...' to learning intentions to help students not only understand what they will be learning but also why. Elder (2012) writes, 'By inserting the connective "So that...", there is a concrete way to communicate the relevance of learning. This can also counter challenges from those students who, when faced with something new or unfamiliar and are reluctant to take an intellectual risk, ask why they need to learn/do/understand/study this or learn in this way.'

Here are two examples of clear, specific and desirably difficult learning intentions that also include 'so that...' as a way to add further purpose and meaning to learning.

Year 7 drama lesson

Learning intention: To understand the importance of gesture, movement and facial expression in communicating meaning to an audience so that you can perform confidently and realistically.

Year 7 geography lesson

Learning intention: We will investigate settlement shapes using an Ordnance Survey map so that you have successfully used a map to pinpoint different settlement shapes.

It is also a useful idea to link the learning intentions to what students already know. Graham Nuthall, author of the excellent book *The Hidden Lives of Learners* (2007) revealed that through his extensive research he discovered, 'students can be busiest and most involved with material they already know. In most of the classrooms we have studied, each student already knows about 40-50% of what the teacher is teaching.' Some students will know things that their peers don't and the learning intention, therefore, can be difficult to pitch as different students can have different levels of background knowledge and understanding linked to it. Teachers should aim to find out what students know or don't know before progressing further.

Key questions to consider when creating and sharing learning intentions:

- What do my students need to know?
- What do my students already know?
- How can I help my students learn what they need to learn?
- How can I check if my students have learned what they should know?

When should learning intentions be shared and explained with the class?

It tends to be standard classroom practice and routine to start lessons sharing and explaining learning intentions but Wiliam and Leahy (2015) identify and explore three key reasons why starting every single lesson with a learning outcome can be potentially a bad idea.

1. Wiliam and Leahy write, 'First, sometimes you don't always know exactly where the lesson is going.' Every teacher can relate to this and actually, a lesson may require completing a task or assessment from a previous lesson so it simply wouldn't make sense to explain the learning intention then revisit previous learning, to then again return to the learning intention shortly after. There are a host of reasons, known to teachers, why starting a lesson with the learning intention may not be the best option and we use our professional judgment to decide that.

2. They also add, 'Second, sometimes telling students where you are going spoils the journey.' I like this point a lot as it illustrates the excitement and curiosity that lend themselves so well to learning new content.

3. Finally, Wiliam and Leahy add, 'Third, and perhaps most important, starting every lesson with a learning outcome is a recipe for uninspired and uninspiring teaching. Those who mandate starting every lesson with a learning outcome forget one important, and universal, fact about schools: not all children are motivated.' Absolutely. There is no doubt that learning intentions are important and should become embedded as a staple classroom routine but this does not need to be rigid.

Case study: The enquiry approach with learning intentions

An enquiry question – often referred to as key or big questions – has to be motivated by a learning intention. Without a clear learning intention (clear to the teacher at least) there is no way to judge whether a particular question is worth asking. Principal of The Duston School and author of Education Exposed, *Samuel Strickland has explained why he is an advocate for this approach and how he has led this across his school with the use of 'Big Questions'.*

In essence, a Big Question is a hook for a lesson or sequence of lessons. Their effective use encourages pupils to explore a problem, drawing on substantive subject-specific knowledge. If they are used effectively then they will bring about a neat interplay of the core (the stuff/knowledge) that pupils need to know and the hinterland (stories, frames and hooks) upon which to hang that core disciplinary knowledge. If anything, they are integral to a knowledge-rich approach.

If I were to pose a challenging Big Question to my class, for example, 'How significant was the role of propaganda in Hitler's rise to power?' then I am going to draw upon a very clever interplay of long-term knowledge (what is in the pupil's schema) and present brand-new material. This material will then be carefully presented, scaffolded and modelled. I will also need to ensure that students have a confident grasp of the terminology included in the 'Big Question', so for this example, it would be the understanding of Nazi propaganda. The ultimate aim is that the pupils can produce an end product. In this example, I am also coaxing my pupils to consider a deeper subject-specific disciplinary skill, i.e. to consider 'how far'. This is by no means easy and is a highly sophisticated thing to do and likely to extend further than one singular lesson.

Some Big Questions can span multiple lessons. Some lessons do not need them. Some lessons are pause lessons. Some lessons are assessment lessons. Staff can use their own professional judgement. I am very clear about the approach I want to see. I want to see my staff welcoming students at the doors of classrooms, giving students a retrieval quiz to undertake as a settler. All lessons should then have a clear hook, i.e. a Big Question.

You can follow Samuel Strickland on Twitter @Strickomaster.

I have written extensively about retrieval practice, the act of regularly recalling information from long term memory in order to enhance learning. 'Big Questions' can be referred to in future lessons as a free recall retrieval task. After time has passed, this can consist of lessons or weeks, a Big Question can be posed again but not with an enquiry focus but instead the focus shifting to recalling information from long term memory. As stated above with learning versus performance, learning intentions must be long term and will need to be revisited after time has passed to ensure learning has taken place.

The grid below shows a retrieval grid which contains four 'Big Questions' from across a term. This is where interleaving and spaced retrieval practice can be combined with learning intentions. This can be delivered at the start of a lesson and then linked to the 'Big Question' set during that lesson. The number of questions can vary on how much content you want students to recall. An icon or image could also be included as a picture prompt for cued recall.

Big Questions: Retrieval practice grid

What were the aims of the 'Big Three' with the Treaty of Versailles?	What were the key military terms of the Treaty of Versailles?
What were the economic effects of the Treaty of Versailles on Germany?	How did the Treaty of Versailles help Hitler rise to power?

Reminder

Big Questions should also be:

1. Clear
2. Specific
3. Desirably difficult

Keep the context of learning out of the learning intention

Although I advise making learning intentions specific, this is only to a certain point as a learning intention shouldn't contain the context of learning. This is excellent and sound advice provided by Shirley Clarke and is also shared by Wiliam and Leahy. When I initially read this, I was unsure as to why or how this was a bad technique but it quickly became clear to me. This is an example of the context of the learning being used as a learning intention:

> *To be able to write a clear set of instructions as to how to make a lasagna dish.*

Instead, the learning intention should remove the context (in this case, the lasagna) so that it is transferable to another context.

> *To be able to write and lay out a clear set of step-by-step instructions.*

This can then be applied to lots of other different and relevant contexts rather than limited to lasagna! The success criteria used for this also shouldn't focus on the context of the lasagna but instead the task and challenge of being able to write a clear set of instructions.

Success criteria in action in the classroom

Learning intentions are descriptions of the intended change in long-term capability. Success criteria are descriptions of desired performance in learning tasks. In other words, learning intentions and success criteria differ not in their specificity, but in what they refer to. The distinction is important because learning is a change in long-term capability, so learning cannot be judged in the moment. That's where success criteria come in.

Success criteria are the manageable breakdown of the learning intentions to help the student achieve the desired goal in terms of content, skills and/or knowledge to be learned. It goes without saying that the learning intentions and success criteria must be explicitly linked and the students should know and be aware of this too. Success criteria can also allow students to monitor their own progress and assess their success. It can also show students explicitly what success looks like through modelling and worked examples (Wagoll – What a good one looks like). Showing the final product in the early stages can be incredibly helpful for students. Hattie (Lori Loehr, 2015) has stated that the best way to show students what success criteria look like is to simply show them, show them what an A or B grade looks like before they start, and show them what the end of the product looks like.

If you haven't viewed the video with educator Ron Berger entitled Austin's Butterfly (EL Education, 2016) then I highly recommend you do so. That clip shows not only the power of peer feedback but also how students can be inspired by the work of their peers too. When sharing the work of others, it is advisable to anonymise the student's work being shared. Over the years I have collected a bank of examples that I share with my students and one of the first questions asked is, 'Who did that Miss?'. Anonymity can keep the focus on the work rather than on the student that produced the work.

Tips for sharing success criteria with students

Co-construct	Have an outline of the required success criteria then co-construct them with students together, although we cannot simply let the students decide what counts as good work or not. Simply presenting success criteria to students runs the risk of them not understanding the criteria and, therefore, it won't have a positive impact on their learning and progress. This strategy can support and promote a learner's independence, as well as providing a sense of ownership over their learning and progress.
Generic success criteria	There can be generic success criteria for all written based tasks because we know as teachers how frustrating it can be when students forget basic literacy skills, such as using capital letters and full stops correctly. A literacy mat with basic rules can be created and shared with students to remind them and for them to refer back to during different stages of the process, once again encouraging independence and reflection.
	Shirley Clarke has written extensively on how success criteria can be used effectively to support learners with their learning but every teacher needs a plan to take the scaffolding away as scaffolding the student's work can improve performance but not the learning. Clarke (2009) writes, 'Once children have success criteria, they have a framework for a formative dialogue, with other peers or teachers, which enable them to:
	- Ensure understanding
	- Identify success
	- Determine difficulties
	- Discuss strategies for improvement
	- Reflect on progress'
Collaborate with others	As with learning intentions, it is a useful activity to view other examples of success criteria, particularly within the same subject, either at a department level or working with subject and phase communities. It is important to reflect on the use of success criteria. Are they being used across the department? Are they being used across the school? Are they having a noticeable and positive impact on learning, progress and outcomes? Are students in your class confident using success criteria and do they understand how to use them to support and aid their learning?
Learning first	Just as learning intentions can become lethally mutated so can success criteria. We need to avoid them becoming a tick box or checklist that students don't actually refer to or engage with but instead support learners making progress and achieving success.

Summary

- Learning intentions and success criteria both play an important role in the planning and learning process for both teachers and students.

- Learning intentions and success criteria have the potential to hinder rather than help learning, if mutated and enforced in ways that waste time, becoming a tick box activity and detracting from long-term learning.

- Learning intentions should always be designed so that they are clear, specific and desirably difficult.

- It is essential learning intentions and success criteria are communicated with clarity for all learners in the classroom.

- Learning intentions don't always need to be designed for a single lesson. Instead, we should use retrieval practice to check the learning of the stated learning intention at a later date. Success criteria will refer to different stages in the learning process and this should not be limited or restricted to a single lesson, being aware of learning versus performance.

- Differentiate success criteria, not learning intentions.

CHAPTER 2

ENGINEERING EFFECTIVE CLASSROOM DISCUSSIONS AND ACTIVITIES THAT ELICIT EVIDENCE OF LEARNING

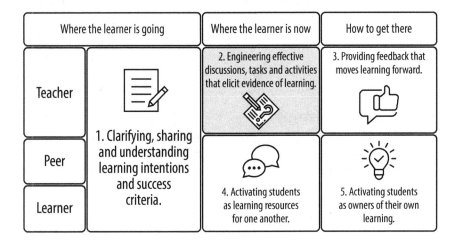

What do Wiliam and Leahy say about eliciting evidence of learning?

- 'To teach well, we have to find out what students already know. But students do not always learn what we teach. That's why finding out what students do know is essential to good teaching.'

- 'Finding out what learners know is difficult for two main reasons. First, in many subjects, the evidence has to be sought. We can't peer into a student's brain and see why he or she is having difficulties understanding texts, for example. We have to go looking for the information. Even in so-called practical subjects, working out what is going wrong requires expertise.'

- 'Second, students are often reluctant to share their thinking – it is a source of some mystery to many teachers why students are so reluctant to allow teachers to see their scratch work. It may be tempting to view this as a problem for the student, but actually, it's more of a problem for the teacher. You can't do your job unless you find out what your students already know.'

- 'We believe that the best way to find out what students are thinking is by talking to them.' (Wiliam and Leahy, 2015)

This chapter covers what I consider to be at the heart of great teaching and learning; finding out what our students have learned and what they can or can't do yet. This is absolutely fundamental to ensuring our students are making progress and to guide our next steps and future planning. Eliciting evidence of learning has been described by Wiliam (Dylan Wiliam, 2020) as one of the most powerful strategies with formative assessment.

A misconception teachers can have in terms of this element of formative assessment is that it solely focuses on questioning. Questioning is central and very important when it comes to eliciting evidence of learning but it is only one of many techniques in our teaching and learning toolkit to help us do this.

Questioning in the classroom

At my school, we have four areas of focus for teaching and learning across the whole school. These priorities are literacy, cognitive science, feedback and questioning. The foci have been the same for three years as we have worked on doing the same but better. Regardless of whether the lesson is taking place in a physical or virtual classroom, questioning plays an essential role in every lesson. Wiliam states that the main concept and idea is that questioning should simply cause thinking and/or provide us useful information to help us teach better (Dylan Wiliam, 2020).

There are benefits of using both closed and open questions in the classroom as a form of eliciting evidence of learning. Here are some examples of closed, open and higher-order questions in English:

Closed question: *Where did Romeo meet Juliet?*

Open question: *Why does Romeo kill Tybalt?*

Higher-order question: *How do Romeo and Juliet change throughout the play?*

Higher-order questions will naturally require more thinking time and these are questions that we should share, discuss and work on with our colleagues. Wiliam offers this simple advice to teachers when asking higher-order questions.

Plan it	Ask it	Be quiet

I haven't always planned questions carefully and provided enough wait time, either moving on to another student, providing prompts or even answering the question myself! The following pyramid task I created can be used during the attention, encoding and consolidation stage of learning or at a later date, once some forgetting has occurred, from memory as a retrieval task. This resource has a scaffolded approach to questions building up from factual recall and closed questions to higher-order questioning. For this task, students receive more points for answering more complex questions but I instruct students to start at the bottom and work their way up to higher-order thinking.

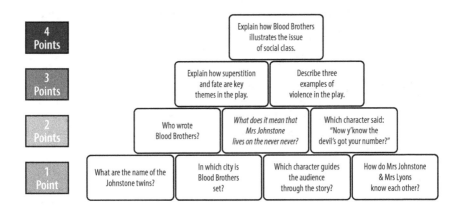

'No hands up, except to ask a question' technique in action

When only a few students are asked questions and volunteer answers, this is a common occurrence and weakness in the classroom. Teachers can encourage (or even at times resort to pleading) with other members of the class to get involved but the struggle is real. There will be confident students that can be relied on to enthusiastically raise their hands, provide and explain correct responses, and then there are other students who are more than happy to let their peers answer and respond on their behalf.

I initially assumed questioning was something all teachers just did naturally, improving over time. In some respects, this is true but this is a slow and ineffective way for teachers to learn and develop. Improvements can happen at a quicker pace if there is genuine support in place, honest reflection carried out and developmental feedback is regularly provided. Also, questioning plays such an important role in the classroom that it is something we should be focusing on getting right as soon as we can, then continue to reflect and refine.

Wiliam and Leahy (2015) have discussed the potential problems with students raising their hands to answer questions as well as the benefits of promoting a 'no hands up, except to ask a question' policy in the classroom. They write, 'If the aim of questioning is to help the teacher find out what the students know, it makes little sense to select a respondent from the volunteers because, generally, students raise their hands only when they are confident they have the correct answer'.

They further add that (Wiliam and Leahy, 2015), 'This is why having students raise their hands to show that they have an answer is such an ineffective technique, even though it is almost universal. Instead, if the teacher is asking the question, it should be the teacher who selects the student or students to respond, ideally, at random. It does make sense to encourage students to raise their hands if they want to ask a question, and this is why we call the basic technique: "No hands up, except to ask a question".'

It's important to understand that a no hands up approach shouldn't result in a chaotic classroom with shouting out and disruption. Various questioning techniques, combined with behaviour management strategies, can ensure effective checking for understanding and can involve all – not some – of the learners in the classroom.

'Cold calling' in the classroom

There are lots of connections and similarities between strategies that Wiliam and Leahy promote and that of teacher and author Doug Lemov, author of *Teach Like A Champion*. A well-known approach promoted by Lemov is 'cold calling'. This is a no hands up questioning method that the teacher can regularly use in lessons. The class will know that they could potentially be asked a question during the lesson. This keeps the learners engaged, prepared and ensures they are paying attention as they are actively involved in class discussions. Below are some simple tips for using cold calling in your classroom:

Know and use student names	Ask another question	Keep it positive	Make time for wait time
Make it the norm in your classroom	Observe others cold calling	Seek feedback on your cold calling	Be clear, specific and desirably difficult

- **Know and use student names:** This technique is best used once the teacher learns the names of all the students in the class (the challenge varies considerably from primary teachers who are with their students on a daily basis to some secondary teachers that may see hundreds of students once a week, context is key). This is more personal than pointing at students and clear pronunciation of names is important too. Cold calling can be warm, in that it is carried out in a safe and inclusive classroom. At the start of an academic year when I am meeting new classes and students, I instruct them to wear a sticky label with their first name written clearly so that it can support me to refer to them by name, as well as helping me learn names quicker.

- **Ask another question:** Make a point of returning to a student you have recently asked to respond, so the class knows they cannot switch off once they have been asked a question as they need to stay focused throughout the lesson.

- **Keep it positive:** It should never appear like we are trying to catch students out. Although students are being held to account with this technique, it should never be used to humiliate or embarrass. Cold calling is a great opportunity to provide genuine praise and encouragement to students or even interest, for example saying to a student, 'I'm really interested in what you might have to say on this topic.'

- **Make time for wait time:** Don't forget to pause, allowing some wait and thinking time for the students. This can be easier said than done so try to be mindful of this when cold calling.

- **Make it the norm in your classroom:** Make cold calling a regular classroom routine. It's even better if it becomes the norm across the whole school as part of the teaching and learning culture.

- **Observe others cold calling:** It can be helpful to watch other teachers carry out cold calling. This can be your colleagues or there are plenty of examples online you can view. There are blogs and videos that explore cold calling on Lemov's website teachlikeachampion.com.

- **Seek feedback on your cold calling:** Another useful idea is to ask an observer to give you feedback about your cold calling questioning – perhaps you aren't providing enough thinking time or are targeting the same students without realising it, as you suspect they will have the correct answer.

- **Be clear, specific and desirably difficult:** As with learning intentions, all questions asked should be clear, specific and desirably difficult, as illustrated in Chapter 1.

Encouraging students to SHAPE their verbal answers

Oracy plays an important role in the study of any language, particularly when students are learning a new language. We want our students to be able to confidently articulate and communicate their opinions and knowledge across all subjects verbally, as well as through their writing.

Barry Smith is a teacher of Modern Foreign Languages (MFL) and executive headteacher. Smith has a strategy that he uses with his students where he tells them to 'SHAPE' their verbal answers, as explained in the summary:

Get students to SHAPE their verbal answers:

- Sentences – no single word answers, use full sentences.
- Hand away from mouth – be confident with your response.
- Articulate – don't mumble or hesitate.
- Project – a loud, clear response that everyone in the class can hear.
- Eye contact – try to maintain this with the teacher or peers.

'SHAPE' encourages students to develop their answers, elaborating on their points and do so with confidence. As with everything in education, as stated previously, context is key. There will be students who this can come very naturally and others that may struggle, especially SEND learners with aspects such as maintaining eye contact. This is where our knowledge of our students is essential. When carrying out cold calling we can also be encouraging students to SHAPE their verbal answers as best they can.

Elaboration

Elaboration has gained a profile in education in recent years as it is an evidence-informed strategy shown to enhance learning and recall. Learning Scientists Megan Sumeracki (formerly Smith) and Yana Weinstein (2016) explain that 'elaboration involves making connections among ideas you are trying to learn and connecting the material to your own experiences, memories, and day-to-day life', and they further add: 'Engaging in elaborative interrogation also encourages you to think about relationships between different ideas, and understanding how two ideas are both similar to one another and how they are different from one another can improve your understanding of the material.'

A useful technique for exploring elaboration is the use of the 5 Ws, although this will depend on the context and topic. Asking further questions such as: When? Where? Why? What? Who? Further elaboration can also be achieved by asking how?

Examples in action in the classroom

An example from the study of history, specifically the Treaty of Versailles:

When was the Treaty of Versailles signed? Put this into context of the period. Who signed the Treaty of Versailles? What can you recall about the individuals involved? Where was the treaty signed? Why was this location chosen? What were the main terms of the treaty? What were the effects of the treaty? What was the reaction to the treaty? Who did the treaty impact the most? Why was the treaty signed? Why was the treaty considered so harsh? What were the short and long-term consequences of the treaty?

An example from the study of physics, specifically the topic of space:

What galaxy is our solar system part of? What is the correct order of the planets? What is a solar system? Why is it not possible to explore the centre of the galaxy? Why is Pluto no longer classified as a planet? When was the status of Pluto downgraded? What do the planets in our solar system orbit and what type of body is it? How many planets make up our solar system?

Elaboration can be combined with many other evidence-informed strategies, such as retrieval and spaced practice, as well as dual coding as shown in the following classroom resource which encourages students to further extend their original explanation.

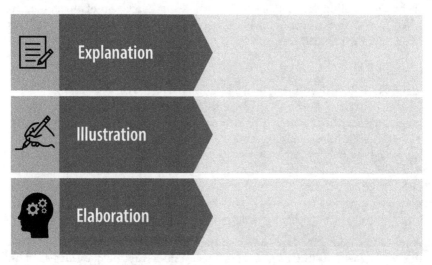

I can recall being frustrated with a class because their responses were very basic and vague. The frustration was due to the fact that I knew they were capable of adding much more detail, depth and explanation to their responses. To show my students how they could do this I gave them short sentences linked to the topic and they had to elaborate on that sentence, extending the initial point further using their own subject knowledge. The example shown also was completed without any support, class notes or textbook as they had to recall that information from memory (I'll discuss more about retrieval practice later in this chapter).

Retrieval Practice: Elaborate and extend

Henry VIII had six wives.	Henry was first married to Catherine of Aragon from Spain, she had previously been married to his brother Arthur before he died. Catherine did not provide Henry with the son he desperately wanted so he wanted to divorce her but that wasn't easy. After he did manage to divorce Catherine he then married Anne Boleyn but she also didn't give him the son he wanted! Anne was executed. His next wife did give him the son he wanted but then she died! Henry went on to have three more wives after this!
Henry VIII broke from Rome.	The break with Rome was linked to Henry wanting a divorce but as he was Catholic he had to ask the Pope for permission and the Pope said no. This led to Henry creating the Church of England and he was known as Head of the Church of England. This was also linked to the spread of Protestant ideas and the work of a German monk called Martin Luther.
Henry VIII dissolved the monastries.	After Henry VIII fell out with Rome he decided to shut down all the monasteries because they were Catholic and he also realised he could make a lot of money from this too! Many people worked and lived in the monasteries so they lost their jobs and homes! This did upset people in England and caused lots of problems. The man that helped Henry with this was Thomas Cromwell.

Mini whiteboards

Mini whiteboards (MWBs) are a classic and useful resource in a teacher's toolkit. They have the potential to be used well to elicit evidence of learning or used badly in the classroom. Ten tips to make the most of these handy resources in your classroom:

1. **Behaviour:** Link usage of MWBs with the behaviour policy. Make it very clear to students what will happen if they write or draw anything that is silly, irrelevant or inappropriate.

2. **Questioning:** Ensure the questions being asked are clear, specific and desirably difficult.

3. **Keep it short:** It is helpful when the questions asked are clear and concise as the answers on the MWBs should be too. When students start writing longer sentences it becomes very difficult for the teacher to quickly scan every response and provide immediate feedback.

4. **Promote literacy:** Remind students you expect them to use capital letters (when appropriate) and spell key terms correctly when using MWBs.

5. **Encourage further elaboration:** One way I do this is by selecting a student, praising their response, which then gives the student the confidence to verbally elaborate on their answer when prompted in a follow-up discussion. I've already told them they are correct so that is their green light to extend their answer and share it with the rest of the class.

6. **Timing:** Think about when to use them and when not to. If you want students to provide a sophisticated, detailed and extended answer then this isn't the right tool to do so.

7. **Dual coding:** They can be used well for dual coding, allowing students the opportunity to combine words and images in their responses. There can also be opportunities where students can illustrate their answers for example a diagram or shape.

8. **Show me:** Make sure all students share and show their responses at the same time with clear 'show me' instructions. This avoids the classic scenario where a student answers first, holds their MWBs up and the rest of the class then takes note and copies (but, of course, the observant teacher can easily spot who is looking around for answers before responding).

9. **Discuss:** Address and tackle incorrect answers and misconceptions. This can be done in a way that doesn't seem like we are targeting someone for answering incorrectly. The incorrect answers also provide us with information we should act on.

10. **Have high expectations:** Students often enjoy using MWBs and view them as fun or informal because their answers can be easily erased away but we should always keep expectations high, even when using MWBs.

Retrieval practice in action

Retrieval is the act of recalling information from long-term memory and retrieval practice is giving students opportunities to practice doing this in order to increase storage strength. The new theory of disuse (Bjork and Bjork, 1992) explains that there are two key measures of memory strength, they are storage strength and retrieval strength. Storage strength refers to how well learned something is and retrieval strength is how accessible (or retrievable) something is.

Retrieval practice is regarded as a powerful teaching and learning strategy. Vast amounts of research have shown it can enhance long-term memory and recall. Wiliam (2020) has noted that 'the benefits of practice testing and distributed practice are two of the most strongly supported learning strategies in all of psychology'. Although it is low stakes and not a formal type of assessment, it is still very insightful in terms of eliciting evidence of learning. Retrieval practice shows very clearly, for both the student and teacher, what the student can recall from long-term memory and gaps in their knowledge.

Retrieval practice should become part of every teacher's classroom routine. As stated in the previous chapter, the start of a lesson is an opportune time to carry out a retrieval task but it should not be limited to a short starter activity. It can be very effective; therefore, we would be foolish to restrict it to just ten minutes at the start of a lesson when it can be used at any point in the lesson.

Ten tips for retrieval practice in action in the classroom

Involve everyone	Vary the retrieval diet	Ensure time for feedback and reflection	Make the level of challenge desirable	Make it time efficient
Specify the knowledge	Make it a classroom routine	Keep it generative	Low effort, high impact	Collaborate with others

1. **Involve everyone:** This is very important because we need to know if all of the learners in our class are making progress and can recall information from long-term memory. This was the main problem with taking a 'hands up' approach to questioning, a wasted opportunity for eliciting evidence of learners from all members of the class.

2. **Vary the retrieval diet:** This variety can include different styles of retrieval from verbal to written. There are also different forms of retrieval too. These include recognition, selecting and identifying the correct answer such as multiple-choice questions, cued recall involves providing support and prompts. Free recall is the most challenging and effortful form of retrieval but the most effective because no support is provided. I encourage teachers to use all of them throughout their lessons. There are also different types of retrieval tasks that can be used – it doesn't just have to be a five-question quiz every lesson!

3. **Ensure time for feedback and reflection:** I was guilty of not doing this properly and thoroughly previously. I would stick answers on the board or instruct students to check their scores without providing time for meaningful reflection to identify and address gaps in knowledge.

4. **Make the level of challenge desirable:** We should allow opportunities for retrieval success and this can also boost confidence and motivation but there must be retrieval challenge and effort too.

5. **Make it time efficient:** This really can be a difficult balancing act when it comes to retrieval practice. Allowing more than ten minutes at the start of a lesson but also not allowing retrieval practice to completely dominate a lesson when new content needs to be delivered.

6. **Specify the knowledge:** Sherrington (2019a) writes, 'Where appropriate, it's better if students know the set of knowledge any retrieval will be based on, so they can study, prepare and self-check. It must be possible for students to check their own answers which has implications for the way the knowledge requirements are laid out.'

7. **Make it a classroom routine:** Retrieval practice should be taking place every lesson. If students know this and it becomes the norm it will also increase the likelihood of it being perceived as low stakes rather than high stakes.

8. **Keep it generative:** Sherrington (2019a) explains that, 'Students need to explore their memory to check what they know and understand; this means removing cue-cards, prompts, scaffolds and cheat-sheets; it means closing the books and thinking for themselves.'

9. **Low effort, high impact:** This has become my teaching and learning mantra, especially with retrieval practice. When it comes to task design and delivery in the classroom, ensuring low effort for the teacher, in terms of your preparation and workload, but in terms of the student, it has a high impact on learning. If we truly want something to become part of a regular classroom it has to be sustainable.

10. **Collaborate with others:** This is something as a profession we certainly should do more of and Wiliam and Leahy both advocate. Share your tasks and questions with colleagues and ask for their feedback and/or view and discuss the questions they ask their students. This can even be extended beyond your department/phase to subject communities and educators online, Twitter for example. I would also recommend visiting and exploring diagnosticquestions.com.

In the online classroom, retrieval practice can and easily continue to take place. There are plenty of free online quizzing tools that can be used to elicit evidence of learning.

I have three key golden rules that every teacher and leader should consider when using technology for retrieval practice:

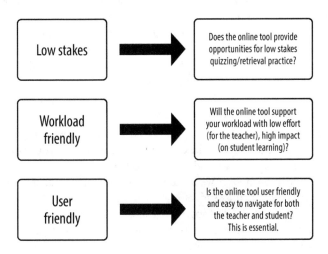

Low stakes	Does the online tool provide opportunities for low stakes quizzing/retrieval practice?
Workload friendly	Will the online tool support your workload with low effort (for the teacher), high impact (on student learning)?
User friendly	Is the online tool user friendly and easy to navigate for both the teacher and student? This is essential.

Multiple-choice questions (MCQs)

A multiple-choice question should contain a stem – the question – and the correct answer and distractors as well as other plausible options. Multiple-choice questioning is a popular form of low stakes quizzing in the classroom. There are a range of benefits in terms of using this quizzing technique and it is useful as eliciting evidence of learning. The success of an MCQ is the question design and not just in terms of ensuring the question is clear, specific and desirably difficult but also the creation of plausible options as distractors. The distractors are the incorrect options provided alongside the correct option, the distractors play an important role as they can determine the challenge of the question.

Designing an effective, challenging and informative MCQ isn't easy and it can be time consuming. The flip side to the workload issue is that MCQs can be very workload friendly in terms of how they are assessed. Based on academic research, discussions with other educators and my own classroom reflections here are some tips for using MCQs:

- **Keep it clear:** In terms of both language and layout. Avoid using complex question styles or answer formats. Complexity can cause confusion, misunderstanding and students can resort to guesswork which doesn't provide us with the evidence we are seeking.

- **Keep it specific:** Ensure that questions focus on specific aspects of knowledge, concepts, content or thought processes that you want to assess and are desirably difficult.

- **Take care using 'none of the above':** If the correct option is 'none of the above' then we may have wasted time and exposed students to a range of incorrect answers. This style of question can be used, although it's not one I use often, so I advise with caution. Sometimes having none of the above makes students choose a wrong answer because they are not confident that all of the answers are incorrect.

- **Take care using 'all of the above':** This can be potentially problematic when 'all of the above' is the correct answer. I thought this strategy would check if students were reading the questions and answers carefully but it can appear as though we are trying to catch the students out. Another potential issue is if a student selects an option that isn't all of the above, this will be classed as incorrect when, in fact, it is a correct answer in addition to the other options, it's just not the answer you were looking for. This needs to be communicated clearly to the learner that their response was correct, alongside all of the others too.

- **Stick to one correct option for younger students:** Take care when asking younger students to select more than one correct answer. Again, this links with the point previously made, as students may select one correct and one incorrect option. Older students, more specifically students at secondary school, can cope with the demands of this question more so. Multiple correct options can be gradated (to engage higher achievers), which makes the likelihood of guessing the correct response lower.

- **Include the option 'I don't know yet':** This links in with the growth mindset approach of not knowing... yet. It also encourages students to be honest and avoid guessing. This can be insightful and reliable for the teacher too in terms of eliciting evidence of learning. Whilst there are many benefits to including this option, it can be problematic, allowing students not to engage by selecting this option every time. Ways to avoid this can be to inform students they have a limit in terms of how many 'I don't know yet' options they can select or it can be removed from some questions.

- **Keep it consistent:** Keep the level of depth for each distractor option the same, e.g., all one word or all extended sentences. More depth for the correct answer can be a giveaway!
- **Allow time for feedback and reflection:** Wiliam has previously stated that the best person to mark the test is the person who has taken it and that certainly applies to an MCQ quiz (Hendrick and Macpherson, 2017, p. 35).

Hinge questions

Building further on the discussion of MCQs are hinge questions. A hinge question is a carefully crafted multiple-choice question with the aim to assess understanding of a key concept. All of the options provided are plausible and feasible that can highlight potential misconceptions and misunderstandings that can arise. Good hinge questions are durable. They will be questions to ask again in the future and are portable, working well in different classrooms. When used as a hinge question, there is no marking at all, simply scanning the responses with self and peer assessment or online tools that do the marking and provide instant feedback for the student and teacher.

Statements to elicit evidence of learning

Teachers can make statements, as an alternative to asking questions, to find out what students know and understand. A powerful and carefully considered statement can encourage debate, discussion and elaboration in contrast to an answer to a set question. Statements can be used to promote verbal discussions in class or form the basis of written tasks, sometimes referred to as 'talking points'.

Examples in action in the classroom

The examples below are statements from across a range of subjects which can promote deep and thoughtful thinking and result in developed responses that will require students to be able to recall relevant information in the context of their learning.

Art: **Charles Mackintosh was the greatest art nouveau designer of his time.**

History: **The main cause of the outbreak of World War One was the assassination of Franz Ferdinand.**

English Literature: **Carol Ann Duffy often presents women as dangerous and destructive.**

Business: A UK business has experienced slow growth in sales in recent years. It has decided to achieve higher growth through new product development – this is a risky strategy.

Case study: Exit tickets to elicit evidence of learning

Jason Chahal is a primary school teacher and the work of Wiliam and Leahy has greatly shaped and influenced his teaching practice. Chahal writes how he uses exit tickets regularly in his lesson as a method of eliciting evidence of learning.

Teachers are forever trying to find ways of finding out what a student has learned in a lesson. More often than not, we would like to think that our instruction was adequate enough for students to have gleaned some understanding of the key concept during the lesson. If this were the case then there would be no need for assessment and we could simply teach the curriculum and record our efforts. This, as we all know, isn't the case. Therefore, we need assessment in order to check for understanding and guide our future teaching – the bridge between teaching and learning. One tool that can help to obtain a snapshot of students' understanding is that of exit tickets. This low-stakes formative assessment tool provides an immediate picture of students' understanding and can act as a gauge of their performance in that particular lesson.

What are exit tickets?

An exit ticket should be a task that is given out near the end of a lesson, which takes students a few minutes to complete. The teacher should use a pre-prepared question that relates to the key concept that was covered in the lesson. Open-ended questions could be used in order to elicit a student's understanding and any possible misconceptions. Avoid using questions relating to self-reporting for example, 'How confident are you about today's lesson?' Exit tickets can check whether a concept has been understood at a single point in time but what they can't check is whether a student can still recall that after a period of time. However, if an incorrect answer is given, we can be sure that the concept has definitely not been understood and if the question that was posed was sufficiently open-ended, we could obtain some misconceptions and use these incorrect responses as distractors for future lessons.

Here is an example of how to use them in class:

Before the end of a lesson, display the question for all to see and hand out individual slips of paper with the same question on them (these are the exit tickets). Make sure the students do not use notes, textbooks or their peers to answer. Get students to write their names on the back of their slips. Make them hand their tickets to the teacher as they leave the lesson.

What do we do with the evidence elicited from the exit tickets?

The data obtained from exit tickets can be very useful and help the teacher decide where to begin the next lesson and tailor their instruction accordingly. Assessments that serve a formative function are validated by their consequences (Wiliam and Black, 1996). This means that the evidence elicited from them should be interpreted and used to make decisions about the next steps in instruction and learning. Wiliam (Wiliam and Black, 2009) states that these decisions 'are likely to be better, or better founded, than the decisions they would have taken in the absence of the evidence that was elicited'. If students fundamentally missed the key concept, it is better to have found out than not to have checked at all. This is where teachers must distinguish between performance and learning.

Teachers will use a range of techniques and questioning to find out where learners are in their learning. Teachers can review written work regularly and walking around the classroom, observing and having conversations are all informal methods of eliciting evidence of student learning. Teachers can easily observe student performance during practical subjects such as drama and physical education and can also monitor progress during design and creation in subjects like art and design and technology. There will be plenty of opportunities in lessons for students to showcase their learning and progress that go beyond answering questions.

Summary

- Eliciting evidence of learning is important and useful. It supports the student and teacher to make informed decisions about the next steps in the teaching and learning process.

- The purpose of questioning should be to make students think and/or to provide the teacher with useful information about what our students know or don't know yet.

- When asking questions that require higher-order thinking don't forget to plan, ask and wait.

- All questions should be clear, specific and desirably difficult in their design and delivery.

- When it comes to asking questions in class, take a 'no hands up, except to ask a question' approach.

- Retrieval practice is an example of assessment for learning and it can be used to effectively and efficiently elicit evidence of learning.

- Multiple-choice as hinge questions are very effective for eliciting evidence of learning when designed, planned and asked carefully.

- Questioning is a very powerful and important method of eliciting evidence of learning but it is not the only way to do so. Statements, elaboration and classroom observations and discussions are also useful techniques.

- Collaborate with colleagues and others in your subject/phase community to design effective questions, activities and tasks that can be used to elicit evidence of learning.

CHAPTER 3

PROVIDING FEEDBACK THAT MOVES LEARNERS FORWARD

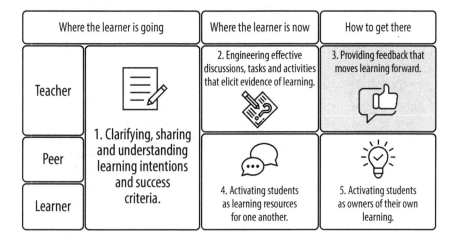

Where the learner is going		Where the learner is now	How to get there
Teacher	1. Clarifying, sharing and understanding learning intentions and success criteria.	2. Engineering effective discussions, tasks and activities that elicit evidence of learning.	3. Providing feedback that moves learning forward.
Peer		4. Activating students as learning resources for one another.	5. Activating students as owners of their own learning.
Learner			

What do Wiliam and Leahy say about providing feedback to move learners forward?

- 'When we elicit evidence about what our students have actually learned, we frequently find out it is not what we wanted them to learn; therefore, we need to provide feedback to get the learners back on track.'

- 'One might assume that since we now have over 100 years of research on feedback we would have some clear answers to the question of what kinds of feedback work best. Unfortunately, this is far from the case.'

- 'The only thing that matters with feedback is the reaction of the recipient. That's it. Feedback – no matter how well designed – that the student does not act upon is a waste of time.' (Wiliam and Leahy, 2015)

Feedback can often seem like a grey area, as Wiliam and Leahy noted the research in this field is complex and at times contradictory. The Education Endowment Foundation (2018a) report: 'Feedback studies tend to show very high effects on learning. However, it also has a very high range of effects and some studies show that feedback can have negative effects and make things worse. It is therefore important to understand the potential benefits and the possible limitations of feedback as a teaching and learning approach.'

The suggestion that feedback can make things worse and hinder learning is very alarming and concerning. Naturally, we want to avoid this, therefore we need to think very carefully about the feedback we provide to our learners to help them move forwards. Students receive feedback on a daily basis in school in various forms and the feedback they receive will vary from subject to subject. As Michael Chiles writes in his brilliant book *The Feedback Pendulum*, 'Feedback is everywhere and plays a pivotal role in learning about ourselves as well as shaping how others perceive themselves.' Feedback is another crucial aspect of formative assessment.

I didn't engage with any research or reading linked to feedback in the early years of my career because I felt this was pointless at the time. No matter what I read or discovered, I had to stick to the school marking policy that was in place. There were guidelines as to how to mark and provide feedback to students and when to do so. This is why it is important not just for the classroom teacher to be evidence informed but also for the whole school culture to build on research so that teachers aren't shackled to outdated and ineffective policies. In recent years, attitudes towards feedback have changed and there is now much more consideration of the impact of feedback on student progress and teacher workload – both factors are important.

At my current school feedback is one of our whole school teaching and learning priorities. Departments have been encouraged to find an approach to feedback that works within our subjects. There are both elements of consistency and flexibility when it comes to whole school feedback at my school. There are many questions that have been asked by teachers and school leaders when it comes to feedback, such as:

Is feedback more effective immediately after or delayed?

Should feedback be specific or general?

Which is more effective – verbal or written feedback?

How often should we provide feedback to learners?

Whilst I will aim to address those questions, we shouldn't become too fixated on them as Wiliam and Leahy (2015, p. 107) state that ultimately 'it comes down to the simple truth that the most effective feedback is just feedback that our students actually use in improving their own learning'. That should be our focus with every piece of feedback provided. Instead focus in schools has previously been on work scrutinies, evidence for senior leaders, parents or Ofsted when in fact we know that the people that it matters most to are the students in our classroom.

The main question we should be considering when it comes to feedback is, 'How can I ensure my students will respond and act on the feedback provided?'

I have summarised a selection of what I consider to be the key pieces of advice offered by Wiliam and Leahy when it comes to feedback to move learners forward:

Trust	Get to know your students well and build their trust as this will support how they receive and react to your feedback.
Take care with the research material available	Wiliam and Leahy (2015, p. 108) promote an evidence-informed approach to teaching and learning but they offer a word of caution to teachers, 'Authors bombard teachers with advice that feedback should be verbal rather than written, immediate rather than delayed, and so on. This advice is certainly correct much of the time, and maybe even most of the time, but it is certainly not true all of the time.' A critical lens and awareness of our context and students are vital.
Build your students' capacities to use feedback	This is ultimately one of our priorities when it comes to embedding formative assessment that students can use the feedback they are given.
Model how to respond and act on feedback	Students need to be explicitly shown this otherwise they can simply read the feedback and not act on it, or, even worse, they may not even engage with feedback provided and ignore it completely.
Growth mindset	Wiliam and Leahy highlight how giving and receiving can be very emotive and personal. A growth mindset can support a positive attitude in terms of students welcoming and embracing feedback to improve. Aim to develop a growth mindset with students in your class. We want our students to warmly welcome feedback.
Link to progress	Help your students see the connection between the feedback and their progress.
Feedback to move forward	Help your students to develop appropriate yet ambitious learning goals. The feedback we provide must be realistic but also challenge students to do better and improve.

Praise	Be careful how and when you offer praise – don't give it too lavishly and often but, instead, when deserved, appropriate and related to things that are within the individual's control.
Personal bests	As an alternative to class ranking and grades, use personal bests for students to focus on when improving.
Design feedback as part of a system	Do not provide feedback on every piece of work that students complete. This is obviously important from a workload perspective but it is not a good use of teacher time either.
Focus on forwards not backwards	Feedback should be focusing on moving the student forward, focusing on what's next instead of what has passed and is done.
Feedback should be more work for the recipient than the donor	This links in with the point above about modelling how to respond and engage with feedback. Teachers shouldn't give feedback unless they allocate time in a lesson for students to respond to that feedback.
Link to learning intentions and success criteria	Focus on the long-term learning and goals, but the short-term feedback should be linked to the learning intentions and success criteria.

Based on the work of Wiliam and Leahy, as well as my own reflections, these are my three important factors to consider when it comes to providing feedback to move learners forward:

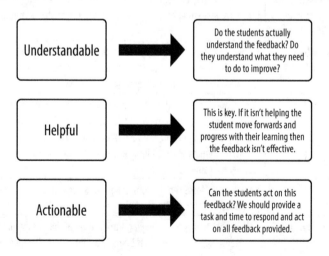

Wiliam's four quarters marking

Wiliam's four quarters marking is brilliantly simple and effective. I embraced it as a teacher and middle leader, as well as sharing it with the senior leadership team at my school.

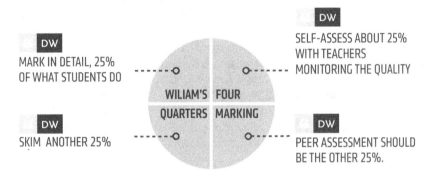

Diagram from Hendrick and Macpherson (2017)

It is a clear concept that can work across different subjects and key stages/ phases. It addresses how often we should be providing feedback and what type of feedback we should be providing. Teachers should mark 25% of what students do in detail, then skim another 25%, students should then self-assess about 25% with teachers supporting and monitoring the quality of that assessment, and finally, peer assessment should be the other 25%, again with support and guidance as to how to do so. Wiliam (Hendrick and Macpherson, 2017, p. 32) describes it as 'a sort of balanced diet of different kinds of marking and assessment'.

What do the four quarters marking actually look like in the classroom? As a department, we have discussed and agreed on which assignments or essays will be marked in detail, this can be moderated too. As head of department, I have found this very helpful and it promotes consistency across classes in the school too. General classwork will be skimmed and scanned to check for understanding, accountability of the students and also to identify areas for development. The other two areas of assessment, peer and self-assessment, seem easy to implement but pose many problems in terms of being done effectively and efficiently by the students. There certainly needs to be a lot of teacher guidance and support provided.

Retrieval practice tasks lend themselves very well to peer and self-assessment, as well as another element of marking not included in the four quarters model such as online marking. This includes tools or websites that will mark and score quizzes for the teacher and then instantly provide the teacher and students with results and feedback. There is further discussion of peer and self-assessment in the following chapters.

Wiliam's four quarters marking offers good guidance about how often we should provide feedback without being prescriptive to a specific time period, for example 'work must be marked every two weeks'. The teacher can put the work into context and use their professional judgement to decide which type of feedback should be provided and when. Chiles (2021) echoes this, 'For feedback to be effective, it should be through a variety of different forms that is part of an ongoing process. It should be something that is not allocated a timescale. For this to happen, teachers should have the autonomy to provide feedback as and when it is needed. For this to happen teachers should be equipped with the strategies that will enable them to recognise when pupils need feedback.'

When introducing this policy in a school, Wiliam (Hendrick and Macpherson, 2017, p. 33) advises, 'I would say first of all, headteachers should lay down clear expectations to parents and say things like, "We are not going to give detailed feedback on more than 25% of what your child does. The reason for that is not because we're lazy. It's because there are better uses we could make of that time. We could mark everything your child does, but that would lead to lower quality teaching and then your child will learn less." Heads have to establish those cultural norms. If a teacher is marking everything your child does, it's bad teaching. It is using time in a way that does not have the greatest benefit for students.'

Feedback in action: Making feedback into detective work

Wiliam (Hendrick and Macpherson, 2017, p. 33) has stated that we should make students respond to feedback with a direct task rather than just presenting them with feedback. The detective technique, originally credited to Wiliam and Leahy (2015), is a great way to do so. This has become one of my favourite feedback techniques. Through using this in my lessons, I have observed the positive impact it can have on student learning and progress. The students are the detectives and have to find out for themselves, with some guidance from the teacher, how they can improve. Students can initially find this technique frustrating. Some would simply prefer the teacher to just tell them where they went wrong and how to fix it whereas this technique requires the students to think hard and carefully to recognise and rectify their mistakes.

If a student has answered ten maths questions but only seven of them are correct, instead of the teacher pointing out which questions are incorrect the teacher can tell the student three are incorrect. The student then has to return to their answers, double-check and find out which three are wrong and correct them – this is the find and fix approach. This technique does require more time and effort from the student but this comes back to the idea that feedback should be more work for the recipient than the donor.

Marking for literacy

Literacy codes/symbols can be very helpful, but obviously, students must be informed of what each code represents so that they can fully understand the feedback and act on it. This will be more effective when used consistently across a department, or even better, across the whole school.

Here is an example of some common literacy codes to use when marking in detail or perhaps skimming written work.

✔	Correct use of literacy and knowledge	P	Check and correct punctuation
Sp	Check and correct spelling	V	Opportunity for vocabulary
Gr	Check and correct grammar	WM	A word or phrase is missing
NP//	New paragraph grammar	WW	Wrong word – homophone e.g., their/they're/there
M	Meaning is unclear or inappropriate language is used	WT	Wrong tense
C	Check and correct use of capital letters	FS	Write in full sentences

Not all feedback should be specific as Wiliam and Leahy (2015, p. 123) point out that 'If the feedback relates only to the particular task at hand, it will improve the student's ability to do that task, but not others, which is not particularly helpful, since the student is unlikely ever to do that task again.' However, I would suggest that, when it comes to literacy, the more specific the better, but again it is important to remember that feedback that improves the work, not the student, is unhelpful. Often teachers write comments such as, 'Take care with punctuation', but this can be vague and unhelpful. This is also another opportunity where the feedback can be made into detective work for the student for example, 'There are three places on this page where nouns should begin with a capital letter.' I would also suggest focusing on one or two key literacy targets at a time, as any more can become overwhelming for the students, whereas one or two allows for the student to narrow their focus on moving their learning forwards by addressing their literacy targets.

Preparing for common misconceptions and mistakes

Prevention is better than a cure and we can apply that concept to teaching, preparing for potential misconceptions and mistakes. After years of teaching the events of 1066 to Year 7 students, I know the key terms that many students will struggle with spelling. These often include: heir, contender, soldier and battle to name a few. Instead of preparing to highlight these mistakes in students' work, I can focus student attention to the spellings of key terms – either with them on display on the board or with a literacy mat on hand for students to refer to. I can prompt the class to check their spellings too. The same can apply to common misconceptions too.

As discussed in the previous chapter, multiple-choice and hinge questions are very useful for addressing misconceptions and provide instant feedback to the correct answers. Author and Director of Education at No More Marking, Daisy Christodoulou (Hendrick and Macpherson, 2017, p. 30) writes, 'Lots of students make similar mistakes to other people in the class and to people who have done the task before, so in a lot of cases you can anticipate the kinds of feedback you should be giving. You can deal with lots of things at once, so I think the way for a teacher to cut down on their workload is to start to anticipate what's going to be a typical response and how they're going to respond to that.' This insight can come from experience and, again, talking to other teachers about how to tackle common mistakes and misconceptions when they arise, or better still, prevent them from occurring if possible – design the teaching to prevent such misconceptions. Some key questions to consider in your subject or phase:

What are the common misconceptions that students often have about this topic?

How can I identify and address this misconception with my class?

What key terms are often challenging to spell?

What other literacy errors are common with this topic/style of task?

Case study: Online feedback

There are many online tools that can help us provide both verbal and written feedback to our classes. I would once again stress that any online tool should be both workload and user friendly. The issue with online tools that improve spelling and grammar is that they automatically correct errors and improve the overall quality of the work but don't necessarily improve the spelling and literacy skills of the learner. This is something for us to be continually aware of and ensure students understand too.

In the following case study from Michael Williams, teacher and head of MFL, he explains how teachers can harness technology to provide feedback to learners. This can be in the physical or virtual classroom with the use of technology.

Most teachers will panic about using online resources to generate feedback, as they feel that nothing will substitute the power of written marking and for their students to be able to flick through their books to see what you have written. Google Docs allowed for easy collaboration between staff and students and this was the first step along the path to giving effective feedback. Students could see my interactions in real time, allowing for more dynamism in the feedback and improvement process, which also led to more interaction on their part to really improve their work. There was an emphasis to take that feedback forward, ensuring the feedback was improving the student not just that piece of work. The quality of student work did improve significantly the more they were exposed to this way of interacting with their work, and this also led to a deeper understanding of success criteria, such as in the drafting of GCSE Spanish responses. Learners knew that if the comments that were being left were to include another tense, they could then refer to that in similar tasks in the future.

Whilst Google Docs was an excellent starting point, I wanted to be able to do more for more students. This led me to explore Kaizena, an add-on to both Google Docs and Slides. Kaizena allowed me to add voice notes to my feedback, which increased the personal nature of the responses. Students could click on my highlighted work and listen to my verbal suggestions and instructions, and once they had completed any improvements, they could also record their answers in the target language, giving me the opportunity to listen to their written work being spoken, thus giving me more opportunities to further help them develop.

Whilst this is excellent for typed work, it doesn't allow for feedback on exam papers and other documents. For this, I always use Kami software, which allows you to edit and annotate PDF documents with typed, handwritten, oral or video responses. The advantage of this is that it makes marking these types of documents very easy, but it is certainly easier when using a device that allows you to use a stylus on the screen. Kami also links really easily with Google Classroom, making integration into lessons, both pre and post-feedback, very straightforward.

Whilst these tools are very useful once work is completed, it can be difficult to generate meaningful feedback opportunities when lessons are being conducted live in a digital environment with remote learning. I really like Pear Deck, which is another Google Slides add-on. It has a library of slides that are ready to use, but essentially you create your slides and build in the interactivity so that you can ask questions and get instant feedback from your class. This allows the normal fast-paced question and answering style of a lesson to be harnessed digitally, which also allows for more realistic teaching to take place. If a student needs a further example or explanation, you will know and be able to act on it instantly, giving you a more meaningful formative assessment that works in an everyday setting.

Five ways of giving effective feedback as actions

This model was created by Tom Sherrington (2017) and contains strategies that can be implemented and embedded in the classroom to encourage students to act on the feedback provided. The 5 Rs of 'action feedback' are:

R1	R2	R3	R4	R5
Redraft or Re-do	Rehearse or Repeat	Revisit & Respond	**Re-learn & Re-test**	**Research & Record**
Go back to edit and improve certain areas of your work.	Go back and practise again and again to master specific skills.	Go back and practise by answering more similar questions.	Go back and make sure you understand previous learning.	Go back and develop your work with deeper insight and wider references.

Taken from Sherrington (2017), originally by @clo_teach

1. **Redraft or re-do:** Sherrington writes, 'Redrafting is very powerful provided that the actions are very specific and the scale of the task is manageable for both teacher and student.' It's so important that students don't view redrafting as simply copying out a piece of work again or focus solely on presentation, making written work look neater the second time. There must be a clear emphasis on making improvements with a redraft. Again, this would be a great opportunity to show how Austin (EL Education, 2016) redrafted and improved his butterfly! A technique is to ask students to highlight in a different colour where they have made the changes/improvements. A redraft should be a different and better piece of work based on the feedback provided.

2. **Rehearse or repeat:** Practical subjects are very good at promoting this but the concept can be applied in academic subjects too. Sherrington (2017) illustrates this by noting that 'any musician will know, the feedback from most instrumental lessons is to practise something specific: some scales, sections of the piece, some finger exercises, a performance, each time paying attention to some very particular skill element for additional fluency.' Musicians and athletes will continue to rehearse and repeat with a continued focus on getting better, we need our students to take this approach to all aspects of their learning.

3. **Revisit and respond:** The key theme throughout this chapter has been ensuring students respond to feedback otherwise what is the point? As Hattie (Chiles, 2020, p. 150) profoundly asked, 'If feedback falls in a classroom and no one hears it, did it make a sound?' In terms of revisit and respond, Sherrington (2017) explained, 'Very simply, this means "do these questions". It could mean going back over fundamentals or being given extension questions. Instead of a commentary on what students have done before, teachers simply issue new questions informed by their reading of student work or their test performances.'

4. **Re-learn and re-test:** Sherrington (2017) states, 'This is very simply a case of specifying a set of knowledge and asking students to return to the routines of retrieval practice.' Retrieval practice allows for immediate feedback, whether that be a quiz, flashcards or a free recall task. A powerful indirect benefit of retrieval practice is that it can clearly and explicitly identify gaps in knowledge. However, this is only powerful if students action this to close those gaps. How can you find out if those gaps have been closed? Further retrieval practice.

5. **Research and record:** Sherrington (2017) addressed how this could but should not be perceived, stating that 'the instruction to "do some more

research" could be horribly unproductive or lead down too many blind alleys. Teachers could specify what reading should be done or where exactly students should research – but also require them to record their findings.' If a piece of work is lacking depth and detail just telling students this isn't very helpful unless we support and guide them as to how they can add more detail. What do they need to add and where can they find this information? Hence, the research and record.

Comment only marking

Students are often accustomed to seeing grades and scores and can be frustrated when these are removed from the feedback. This often isn't easy to introduce because as Wiliam and Leahy (2015) warned, many students don't like comment only feedback. An issue with grades and scores is that students look for the number or letters and can then disregard any comments the teacher has provided. If their score or grade is high then the student is often pleased they have done a good enough job and will aim to do the same next time, although there are very likely still areas for improvement. If a student has a low grade or score, they can feel demoralised, demotivated and disappointed. This can cause a sense of despair and an almost 'what's the point?' attitude. Both of those scenarios are not helpful because, either way, the student isn't engaging and acting on the feedback provided.

In terms of Wiliam's four quarters marking, comment only marking applies best to the 25% of student work that is marked in detail. For example, in my subject at A Level, this will be for an extended essay. I will read the essay closely, perhaps moderate with a colleague and provide detailed comments with my feedback with the expectation that it will be addressed and actioned by my students. This action can involve redrafting or applying the targets to the next essay they complete, but it is important that the feedback isn't forgotten or neglected if time has passed.

There will be times when scores and grades are more suitable, for example a retrieval quiz, but even then, the students should not just look at the score and ignore the gaps in knowledge. If a student achieved 13/15 on a retrieval quiz, they must look at where they went wrong, so the gaps have been identified and can be closed. It can be tempting to stick answers on the board but it is important that time is provided for meaningful reflection with any form of feedback.

Case study: The feedback pendulum

Michael Chiles is the Geography Trust Lead at King's Leadership Academy and author of The CRAFT of Assessment *and* The Feedback Pendulum. *Chiles offers advice to teachers and leaders on effective feedback strategies in action.*

Schools are awash with a frenzy of feedback daily, as Professor John Hattie points out, it could be argued that students are suffering from feedback obesity (Chiles, 2021, p. 149). We shower students with feedback verbally and in written form based on evidence interpreted by teachers from hundreds of assignments, assessments, practice exams, questioning and classroom activities. We direct our students on how to improve their work, correcting them on their behaviour, highlighting where their response may be wrong, or giving them praise for meeting the success criteria based on the learning intentions that have been set. It is difficult to imagine how teaching would be possible without giving feedback.

We give our students lots of feedback, but do they process it appropriately? Is the feedback we are giving them making the sound we intended it to make? I am sure we can all think back to a time when we have given feedback to students but we know it has not been heard. From an early age, we master the art of selective hearing. Even though we freely give feedback until our students are fit to burst, they may not actually receive it as we intended. Or they may just reject it. It is the acting on the feedback that contributes to student's learning. Sharing feedback with students but with no follow-up is like baking a cake and leaving the baking powder out of it but expecting it to still rise nicely. The power of feedback is determined by the power of the follow-up. This was emphasised by Valerie J. Shute's report (2007) on the role of formative feedback, 'good feedback can significantly improve learning processes and outcomes, if delivered correctly'.

So, if we know that the follow up is important in establishing effective feedback and reducing the feedback obesity culture, what can we do as teachers to make this happen? This is not a definitive list but more several suggestions of how we can shift the power of feedback in schools.

Time appropriate

Feedback should be an ongoing process, not something that is time-bound to a straitjacket policy implemented by school leaders. Teachers should be equipped with the strategies that will enable them to recognise when students need feedback. The research points towards applying a delayed feedback approach for encouraging the transfer of learning, while immediate feedback for developing procedural skills.

Culture

Establish an effective culture where students want to embrace the feedback given. No matter how skilful the person is at delivering the feedback, if the person is not willing to listen and absorb the feedback then it will not support learning and, in turn, improvement. Many students would rather be seen as lazy than less intelligent when compared with their peers. Take time to create a feedback pull by establishing positive relationships with your pupils so that they want to engage with your feedback because they know it will help them to improve.

The Goldilocks principle

Create conditions where your feedback is welcomed by not overwhelming your students. If there is too much feedback or it lacks clarity, the next steps can seem unachievable and lead to people pushing back. The feedback provided should be granular, razor-sharp and specific so that the receiver, the pupil or the teacher knows exactly how to improve. It should be clearly linked to the original intentions. They need to feel that the next steps are within their grasp. This, in turn, will make them want to continue to receive more feedback in the future.

Involve everyone

Involve students in the feedback process to support their ability to be able to assess themselves. We should look to create opportunities that build an understanding of their own work through guided feedback. After all, it is only the pupil who can make the necessary changes to their classwork to bring about improvement in learning and, in turn, their performance. Take the time to explicitly teach pupils metacognitive strategies, model your thinking, as well as teaching your students how to manage their learning independently.

You can follow Michael on Twitter @m_chiles.

Summary

- Feedback is a field of research which can be complex and contradictory. It's important to evaluate the context of any given study and keep the focus on providing feedback to move learners forward.

- A strong message Wiliam and Leahy (2015) emphasise is that feedback should be more work for the recipient than the donor.

- Design feedback as part of a system – this is about the importance of feedback, not the intensity of the process and not every single piece of work needs to or should be marked/given feedback.

- Wiliam's four quarters marking is a straightforward, workload friendly and effective strategy for providing various forms of feedback to learners that can be used across departments and phases.

- All feedback provided should be understandable, helpful and actionable.

- There are a range of strategies that are low effort, high impact when it comes to providing feedback, such as the detective strategy.

- It is better for any feedback linked to literacy to be clear, specific and actionable.

- There are a wide range of online tools available to support teacher workload and enable the teacher to provide both verbal and written feedback.

CHAPTER 4

ACTIVATING STUDENTS AS LEARNING RESOURCES FOR ONE ANOTHER

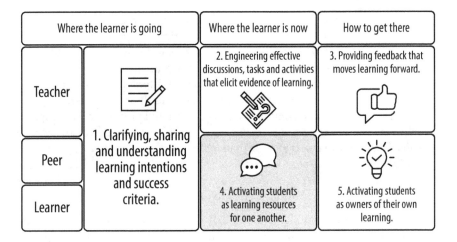

Where the learner is going		Where the learner is now	How to get there
Teacher	1. Clarifying, sharing and understanding learning intentions and success criteria.	2. Engineering effective discussions, tasks and activities that elicit evidence of learning.	3. Providing feedback that moves learning forward.
Peer		4. Activating students as learning resources for one another.	5. Activating students as owners of their own learning.
Learner			

What do Wiliam and Leahy say about activating students as learning resources for one another?

- 'Engaging students in assessing the work of their peers is not just a labour-saving device for teachers. Implemented properly, it can substantially increase student achievement, both for those who get help from their peers, and peers who provide the help.'

- 'Effective cooperative learning requires the presence of two elements. First, there must be group goals, so that students are working as a group not merely working in a group. Second, there must be individual accountability, so that individual students cannot be carried along by the work of others.'

- 'The purpose of peer assessment should be simply, and purely, to help the individual being assessed improve their work.' (Wiliam and Leahy, 2015)

I think this area of formative assessment is possibly the most underused and underestimated by teachers. It certainly has a lot of potential for the classroom. This reluctance can be linked to behaviour issues. We know that when children work together, they can become distracted or distract others. Another common problem with group work is that often one or two students tend to do the work for the rest of the group. Some students view group work or peer collaboration as easy, or a chance to catch up with friends in class but, as Wiliam and Leahy stated, there must be group goals and individual accountability to avoid these issues arising. There are techniques we can implement to ensure students can become effective learning resources for one another.

Why should we be promoting students as learning resources for another? There are a wide range of benefits of peer collaboration, support and assessment. Wiliam and Leahy (2015) explain various reasons why peer collaboration and cooperation in the classroom is so important: 'It is worth noting that there are two rather distinct purposes that people express for cooperative and collaborative learning. The first is that because adults are required to work together in their jobs and communities, schools should prepare young people to work in this way. The second is that having students work together can produce greater learning of subject matter than would be possible by having students work individually or in competition with their peers.' The second factor is more relevant to us as teachers but we do play a key role in preparing students for adult life so both are important factors to be aware of.

There must be a clear understanding that students are supporting their peers with formative and not summative assessment. Wiliam (and Leahy, 2015, p. 137) quite rightly expresses his firm stance on this, 'I think it is quite wrong for one student to be placed in the position of evaluating the achievement of another student for the purpose of reporting to parents or others.' This also relies on the classroom culture. There should be a culture of support and understanding, everyone can make mistakes and everyone can improve. Learning isn't a competition, it isn't a race and formative assessment embodies this, illustrating how learning is an ongoing process.

This idea of collaboration rather than competition is very important. Wiliam and Leahy (2015, p. 141) address this stating, 'Perhaps the most important requirement for effective cooperative learning is that students believe that they are "all in the same boat" so that the success or failure for each individual cannot be separated from those of others in the group. Students are therefore responsible for: (a) making sure that they learn the assigned material, and (b) that the other members of the group also learn the material (what psychologists call "positive interdependence"). This means that there can be no "free riders".' It is essential that we communicate this clearly to prevent this issue of slacking off and relying on others occurring in the classroom.

Case study: Strategies for activating students as learning resources

David Goodwin is a teacher of geography and head of year who regularly promotes and encourages his students to support one another in the learning process.

Wiliam and Leahy declare that short-cycle formative assessment is key to student learning. For the students, this means they benefit from receiving feedback about how well they are doing. For the teacher, they receive feedback about what their students have understood. But how does a teacher give and receive live feedback in a lesson with 30 students? The answer is to have students support each other's learning by training them and using structured routines.

Here are three examples of how I activate students as a learning resource for one another.

Activating students to support one another in deliberate vocabulary development

Most subjects and phases have a notable role to play in developing students' reading confidence. If you want your students' reading confidence to grow, then you need to invest in deliberate vocabulary development. Opportunities to practice the use of tier 3 (subject-specific) and tier 2 vocabulary (sophisticated day-to-day words) should be embedded routinely, in lessons.

Have your students say the words you want them to learn. In pairs, you can have your students discuss the meaning of the words they are learning. Provide structured questions which force students to use the to-be-learned words. Display the questions on a whiteboard (or equivalent device) or print them. The questions could include: 'What does...mean?', 'Can you use the word...in a sentence?', 'Where else might you use this word?' or 'Can you think of a different word which has the same meaning?'.

This technique works because it allows you to circulate the room and monitor what students say to each other. As you survey the classroom, you will identify errors or misconceptions, and ensure discussions remain focused.

Pair share to share the load

Think, pair, share is useful when you are checking for understanding. Therefore, you should frequently use this technique in each lesson. You will find it useful to pre-assign each student's partner. Directing your students to number themselves (1 and 2) will add clarity to your instructions.

Initiate think, pair, share by posing a question for discussion. Wiliam encourages pause time during questioning and it is important to allow time for students to think during this task too before they talk to their peers. Then set a timeframe for how long each student will talk. Signal to the class when it is time for the next student to share their answer. When first using this technique, your students might benefit from you demonstrating how it works. You could also provide prompts, e.g., 'I want you to turn to your partner and begin your answer by saying...'. While students are actively discussing their answers, survey the classroom and monitor students' responses.

Think, pair, share acts as a useful precursor to 'cold call' because students have rehearsed their response. When the teacher decides who answers the question it keeps the whole class involved in thinking. It will also tell the teacher if it is safe to introduce new material. Think, pair, share supports cold call because students feel more comfortable, having rehearsed an answer, to share their understanding publicly.

Paired retrieval

You can train students to support each other in building confidence and fluency. Using a knowledge organiser or equivalent resource, students can quiz each other and use elaborative questioning for retrieval practice. When you have students quizzing each other, use the same routines from think, pair, share: precise time frame, signal the changeover, monitor the room, and follow up with a cold call.

If you want your students to provide expansive answers, then model how to use elaborative questions. The use of elaborative questions involves students in answering: how? Why? What? These sorts of questions explore processes, cause and effect and making predictions.

To get the most out of elaborative questioning, give the students asking questions a resource, such as question stems. You should check for accuracy by monitoring the questioning process. Ensure that, whenever necessary, students in their pairs are providing corrective feedback by referring to their resources.

You can follow David on Twitter @MrGoodwin23 and visit his teaching blog mrgoodwin23.wordpress.com.

Peer tutoring in action

The Education Endowment Foundation (2018c) have featured peer tutoring in their online teaching toolkit. They define peer tutoring: 'Peer tutoring includes a range of approaches in which learners work in pairs or small groups to provide each other with explicit teaching support.' In terms of assessing how effective peer tutoring is as a teaching and learning strategy the EEF reported, 'Overall, the introduction of peer tutoring approaches appears to have a positive impact on learning, with an average positive effect equivalent to approximately five additional months' progress. Studies have identified benefits for both tutors and tutees, and for a wide range of age groups. Though all types of pupils appear to benefit from peer tutoring, there is some evidence that pupils who are low-attaining and those with special educational needs make the biggest gains.'

The EEF (2018c) toolkit further added that 'Peer tutoring appears to be particularly effective when pupils are provided with support to ensure that the quality of peer interaction is high: for example, questioning frames to use in tutoring sessions, and training and feedback for tutors. In cross-age peer tutoring, some studies have found that a two-year age gap is beneficial and that intensive blocks of tutoring are more effective than longer programmes. Peer tutoring appears to be more effective when the approach supplements or enhances normal teaching, rather than replaces it. This suggests that peer tutoring is most effectively used to consolidate learning, rather than to introduce new material.'

These findings further illustrate the research that Wiliam and Leahy refer to about peer collaboration and cooperation as being a low cost and effective strategy to support learning and progress. The EEF recommend that before teachers implement and embed this strategy in their classrooms, they should consider the following key questions:

- Are the activities sufficiently challenging for the tutee to benefit from the tutor's support?

- What support will the tutor receive to ensure that the quality of peer interaction is high?

- Training for staff and tutors is essential for success. How will you ensure sufficient time to train both staff and tutors, and to identify and implement improvements as the programme progresses?

- How will you ensure peer tutoring is being used to review or consolidate learning, rather than to introduce new material?

- Four to ten-week intensive blocks appear to provide maximum impact for both tutors and tutees. Can you arrange for your peer tutoring to follow this structure?

Peer placemat prompts

It can be challenging for students to know what to say to one another in terms of content, feedback and the delivery. I have found the use of placemats, which can be printed and laminated or simply projected onto the class board, to be very helpful. The prompts provide sentence starters and aim to structure the discussions and conversations learners have as well as helping them stay focused. Below is a placemat to prompt verbal discussions between peers with retrieval practice but it can be adapted to focus on feedback prompts, questioning or linked to a specific topic, subject or task.

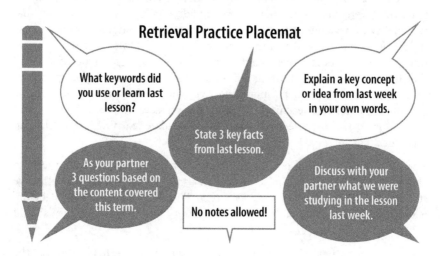

Retrieval Practice Placemat

What keywords did you use or learn last lesson?

Explain a key concept or idea from last week in your own words.

State 3 key facts from last lesson.

As your partner 3 questions based on the content covered this term.

No notes allowed!

Discuss with your partner what we were studying in the lesson last week.

Peer assessment in action

Kind	Specific	Helpful

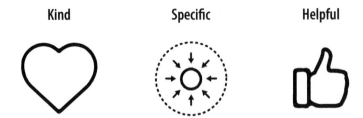

The kind, specific and helpful approach has become widely used in schools and I think it is great. This concept is taken from the work of Ron Berger, author of the superb book *Ethic of Excellence: Building a Culture of Craftsmanship with Students*. All three aspects are important:

Kind: Kindness is key in any school environment and receiving feedback can be very personal and even emotive. It is very important that whilst feedback is honest it is always communicated in a way that is not personal, mocking or cruel but kind. I have read many examples of feedback where students have written or said things to one another such as, 'your handwriting is awful, I can't read it!'. Naturally, this can be very upsetting and negatively impact student confidence and motivation. As adults, whenever we give feedback – either to students or colleagues – we should always be kind too.

Specific: This can be difficult for students to grasp. As mentioned in the previous chapter, literacy targets are often vague and generalised, such as 'Improve punctuation'. This needs to be specific, such as 'Always use full stops at the end of sentences', in order to have an impact on students' progress levels. We must model examples of this in our feedback and when instructing students as to how to give specific peer feedback.

Helpful: Ultimately, all feedback should be helpful with formative assessment otherwise what is the point in receiving the feedback? The more specific the feedback is the more helpful it can be.

Peer assessment is also explored as part of The EEF Teaching and Learning Toolkit. The EEF (2018c) states, 'Peer assessment involves the peer tutor providing feedback to the tutee relating to their performance and can take different forms, such as reinforcing learning or correcting misunderstandings.' A lot of peer feedback on extended pieces of writing tends to take place once a student has completed their work but this is reducing the impact.

English teacher Jamie Clark (@XpatEducator on Twitter) has created the following word diagram for his students to promote the Berger approach to peer feedback. This is very useful and provides clear guidance and support for students as to how they can be kind, specific and helpful in the classroom.

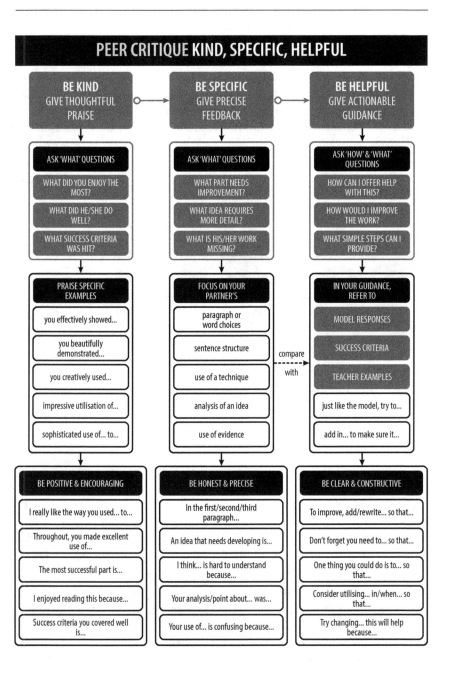

PEER CRITIQUE KIND, SPECIFIC, HELPFUL

BE KIND
GIVE THOUGHTFUL PRAISE

BE SPECIFIC
GIVE PRECISE FEEDBACK

BE HELPFUL
GIVE ACTIONABLE GUIDANCE

ASK 'WHAT' QUESTIONS
- WHAT DID YOU ENJOY THE MOST?
- WHAT DID HE/SHE DO WELL?
- WHAT SUCCESS CRITERIA WAS HIT?

ASK 'WHAT' QUESTIONS
- WHAT PART NEEDS IMPROVEMENT?
- WHAT IDEA REQUIRES MORE DETAIL?
- WHAT IS HIS/HER WORK MISSING?

ASK 'HOW' & 'WHAT' QUESTIONS
- HOW CAN I OFFER HELP WITH THIS?
- HOW WOULD I IMPROVE THE WORK?
- WHAT SIMPLE STEPS CAN I PROVIDE?

PRAISE SPECIFIC EXAMPLES
- you effectively showed...
- you beautifully demonstrated...
- you creatively used...
- impressive utilisation of...
- sophisticated use of... to...

FOCUS ON YOUR PARTNER'S
- paragraph or word choices
- sentence structure
- use of a technique
- analysis of an idea
- use of evidence

IN YOUR GUIDANCE, REFER TO
- MODEL RESPONSES
- SUCCESS CRITERIA
- TEACHER EXAMPLES
- just like the model, try to...
- add in... to make sure it...

compare with

BE POSITIVE & ENCOURAGING
- I really like the way you used... to...
- Throughout, you made excellent use of...
- The most successful part is...
- I enjoyed reading this because...
- Success criteria you covered well is...

BE HONEST & PRECISE
- In the first/second/third paragraph...
- An idea that needs developing is...
- I think... is hard to understand because...
- Your analysis/point about... was...
- Your use of... is confusing because...

BE CLEAR & CONSTRUCTIVE
- To improve, add/rewrite... so that...
- Don't forget you need to... so that...
- One thing you could do is to... so that...
- Consider utilising... in/when... so that...
- Try changing... this will help because...

An example of peer feedback that is kind, specific and helpful

This was from one of my Year 7 classes writing an extended piece answering a big question: Why did William the Conqueror win the Battle of Hastings? We can see, in the example below, that only the first paragraph has been peer assessed as this is what I instructed the class to do, as an important aspect of formative assessment is that it is happening during the learning not bolted on at the end.

The Saxon Gazette   22/11/17

Royal Rumble!   Sp Hastings

Quite recently, King Harold was slaughtered at (Hastigs) as the Saxons fought a tough battle against William the Wonderful and his army.

⊕ Good bias/
Alliteration

Ⓣ check key words
Ⓣ too short and not so detailed

= good
= fix it

                              in January   There
This all started when Edward/the Confessor died since he did not have a heir to the throne ~~their~~ there was a fuss about who would be the next King of England. Apparently Harold was supposed to be king since the late Edward promised him the throne. But everyone knows William the Wonderful should be king!

The student providing feedback has identified that their peer has incorrectly spelt the key term Hastings – writing 'Hastigs' – and used the literacy code 'sp' to do so. The fact that this has been highlighted means that, for the rest of the essay, the student writing it will now be aware how to spell Hastings correctly. If the peer assessment had taken place once the essay was completed, it is likely the student would have continued to write 'Hastigs' throughout. This is very powerful as it is immediate feedback that the learner can respond to and appreciate.

The feedback provided by the student also encouraged more detail, and whilst this could be more specific, we can see the student did make more of a conscious effort to include more detail in the second paragraph. Not only did the students improve their first paragraph, but they were also able to continually improve with ongoing and regular feedback from their peers.

I remember one of the Year 7 boys saying, 'Can you look at this paragraph for me now?' and this simple moment was amazing to observe. The students were valuing the support they could give one another and asking for more feedback!

In terms of the colour coding and use of good/fix it, this was language chosen by the student. Whilst there isn't anything wrong with 'What Went Well', 'Even Better If' and other similar phrases, they simply aren't how students communicate with one another. I don't have a set phrase students must use when providing peer feedback. I will provide guidance and prompts but as long as feedback is kind, specific and helpful then I am happy for them to articulate this clearly.

Wiliam and Leahy (2015) offer useful advice about the use of post-it notes as an alternative to annotations in ink, for both teacher and peer feedback. Some students can regard comments by others as a sign that their work is not good enough or they could be unhappy to see the writing of someone else who has altered their piece and/or tarnished their presentation. Wiliam and Leahy suggest that students write their peer feedback on self-adhesive post-it notes. If the recipient does not find the feedback helpful, they can peel off the notes and discard them or act on the feedback but not feel that their work has been tainted.

It can be very frustrating as a teacher when children say their peers have spelt a key term incorrectly when in fact they spelt it correctly in the first place! It is always worth emphasising the importance of peer feedback but it does take time for students to grasp so, as students are practising this, the post-it notes are a great idea, especially in the early stages of embedding this strategy while the teacher is still responsible for the quality of peer support taking place. Patience and perseverance is often needed from both the teacher and students.

Case study: Promoting peer assessment in the classroom

Victoria Hewett is a geography teacher and author of Making it as a Teacher: How to Survive and Thrive in the First Five Years. *Hewett is an advocate for promoting effective peer assessment in the classroom and she explains how she has done this in her lessons successfully.*

Despite what many feel, I absolutely love using peer assessment with my students. However, to develop effective peer assessment, it is important to model and exemplify what good feedback looks like and train students in the art. This can easily be done through modelling and scaffolding techniques similar to those you may apply to student work.

At the beginning of every year, as I meet my new classes, I take the time to explicitly teach peer assessment strategies and how to give feedback effectively. With Key Stage 3 (KS3) students, I'll try several approaches with them, encourage them to evaluate each technique and then discuss why I choose to use ACE peer assessment as our primary strategy:

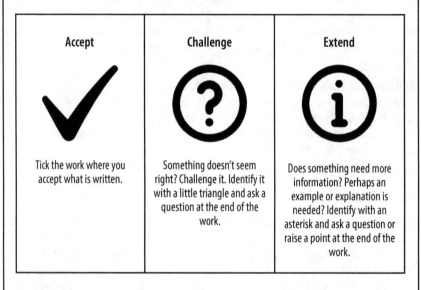

Accept	Challenge	Extend
Tick the work where you accept what is written.	Something doesn't seem right? Challenge it. Identify it with a little triangle and ask a question at the end of the work.	Does something need more information? Perhaps an example or explanation is needed? Identify with an asterisk and ask a question or raise a point at the end of the work.

I find that explicitly teaching peer assessment and feedback helps my students to take ownership and responsibility for the feedback they give and receive.

As with any feedback, it is important that after peer assessment students have time to read, discuss and act on the feedback given. For example, with my KS3 classes, I often use 'pause, peer assess, progress' mid-way through an assessed task. I do this for several reasons, firstly to encourage students to make regular use of the success criteria, then to allow them to find inspiration from others and, finally, to encourage students to proofread and edit as they go. In older year groups, I tend to apply a 'stop, self-assess, progress' approach. This should be ongoing, not to just focus on performance but instead the long-term learning.

I tend to avoid using peer assessment at the end of summative work and never use it to provide students with a final grade. Sometimes I ask exam classes to predict the grade or marks they think a finished piece of work might achieve using a mark scheme and justify their predictions. Doing so is an opportunity for students to engage with the assessment criteria by which they are assessed.

ACE peer assessment encourages students to consider the content of what they assess and their understanding of it in order to identify the elements they accept and agree with, any elements they wish to challenge as an error or misconception and what could be done to extend the piece of work. I usually use ACE feedback whilst students are working on an extended piece of writing or a prolonged task, to allow them to gain feedback and make improvements before they submit their final piece. This technique of accept, challenge, extend can also be applied to class discussions and questioning in that students are encouraged to justify why they accept a previous comment or answer, or they can extend on what has been said or challenge it using their knowledge and understanding.

You can follow Victoria on Twitter @MrsHumanities and visit her teaching blog mrshumanities.com.

Wiliam (and Leahy, 2015, p. 144) has stated that 'Activating students as learning resources for one another can, therefore, be seen as a stepping stone to students becoming owners of their own learning.' Cue the next chapter, the final piece in the formative assessment puzzle.

Summary

- There should be group goals and individual accountability for any peer collaboration to be successful and effective.
- The research linked to peer collaboration and cooperation is positive but the delivery in the classroom isn't always effective as there are several barriers to overcome.
- Peer feedback should always be kind, specific and helpful based on the brilliant advice from educator Ron Berger.
- It is vital we continue to provide opportunities for students as learning resources for one another in the virtual classroom.
- Peer feedback and assessment should not be used for any form of summative assessment.

CHAPTER 5

ACTIVATING STUDENTS AS OWNERS OF THEIR OWN LEARNING

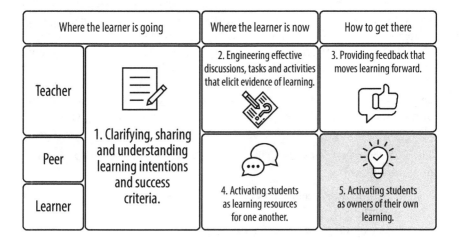

	Where the learner is going	Where the learner is now	How to get there
Teacher	1. Clarifying, sharing and understanding learning intentions and success criteria.	2. Engineering effective discussions, tasks and activities that elicit evidence of learning.	3. Providing feedback that moves learning forward.
Peer		4. Activating students as learning resources for one another.	5. Activating students as owners of their own learning.
Learner			

What do Wiliam and Leahy say about activating students as owners of their own learning?

- 'The curious task of teachers is to work toward their own redundancy. Not literally, of course, because there will always be new students, but for each of our students, we should be working toward a situation where our students need us less and less.'

- 'No matter how much our students learn in our classrooms, if they leave school with the passion for knowledge extinguished, we will have failed them. That is why the fifth and final strategy is in many ways the most important – the one that the other four strategies have been leading up to.'

- 'When students are owners of their own learning, all the other strategies fall into place.' (Wiliam and Leahy, 2015)

This strand of formative assessment really is the holy grail of teaching and learning. I, like many other teachers, have invested a lot of time, effort and energy promoting effective study strategies with the aim that students will become equipped with the knowledge and skills to use these strategies independently to become lifelong learners. Self-regulated learning and metacognition are terms and concepts that are becoming more mainstream and widely known in education now.

The EEF toolkit has an informative guidance report dedicated to metacognition and self-regulation. The report (Education Endowment Foundation, 2018b) states, 'Metacognition and self-regulation approaches aim to help pupils think about their own learning more explicitly, often by teaching them specific strategies for planning, monitoring and evaluating their learning.' The report also stresses the effectiveness of metacognition and self-regulation as the approaches are described as having 'consistently high levels of impact, with pupils making an average of seven months' additional progress'. This again emphasises why teachers and students need an awareness and understanding of the benefits and how they can be applied to support learning but this isn't always easy for students to grasp.

The EEF report explains that self-regulated learning can be divided into three main components:

- Cognition: the mental process involved in knowing, understanding and learning.
- Metacognition: often defined as 'learning to learn'.
- Motivation: willingness to engage our metacognitive and cognitive skills.

Motivation is incredibly important and much has been discussed, explored and written around this subject in education, as we would expect. There has been a noticeable shift in terms of how, as a profession, we view motivation in the classroom, based on the work of influential academic researchers such as Nuthall (2007). This is summed up well by Carl Hendrick (2017) who wrote that 'motivation doesn't always lead to achievement, but achievement often leads to motivation.' Instead of investing time creating displays with motivational quotes and posters, our efforts should be fully invested in ensuring that our students make academic progress and the knock-on effect of this will be increased motivation to further succeed and grow.

Wiliam and Leahy (2015, p. 186) write about motivation: 'In education, it is routinely assumed that intrinsic motivation is better than extrinsic motivation – indeed, extrinsic motivation is routinely equated with punishments, blandishments, and rewards, while intrinsic motivation is portrayed as pure and unsullied. As we will see, things are a little more complicated than that, and we believe that there is a clear and important role for both intrinsic and extrinsic motivation in helping students become owners of their own learning.' Students achieving success, progress and receiving helpful feedback and genuine praise can all be extraordinary motivating factors for them to take ownership of their own learning.

Throughout this book, I have referenced the work of Bjork and Bjork (2011) and their theory of desirable difficulties – providing an appropriate and desirable level of challenge for students. This is also central to motivation because if tasks and work that are set prove too easy or too challenging then that can have a negative impact on their levels of engagement, enthusiasm and motivation. When the level of challenge is desirable and success is challenging but possible that can provide motivation for learners to progress.

The EEF (2018b) guidance report notes that 'self-regulated learners are aware of their strengths and weaknesses, and can motivate themselves to engage in, and improve, their learning'. An awareness of strengths and weaknesses, once again, comes from a combination of the formative assessment strands such as students knowing what they should be learning, how to get there with teacher and peer feedback provided along the way to reach a stage of confidence and independence.

There have, once again, been many misconceptions around this strategy, including suggestions that this means lazy teaching and leaving students to do their own thing, which we know is far from the truth. To ensure students take responsibility and ownership for their learning (and do so effectively) requires a lot of planning, explanation, modelling, instruction and support from the teacher as well as investment, attention and effort from the student. As Wiliam and Leahy (2015) stated, all of the other strands of formative assessment ultimately lead to this point. An understanding of the learning intentions, use of success criteria and feedback from teachers and peers all contribute to the point where a student feels confident and ready to take ownership of their own learning. This does take time and requires a lot of hard work, from both the teacher and student.

An issue – and a big one at that – is that even those students that are eager to take ownership of their learning often don't know how to. This is why the role of the teacher modelling techniques with explicit guidance is so important. The research summary, *Strengthening the Student Toolbox* by Professor John Dunlosky, is an excellent resource for sharing effective evidence-informed study strategies with colleagues, students and their families. Highlighting, underlining and re-reading tend to be study techniques that students favour perhaps because they are common practice, require minimal effort and lack challenge. In this summary Dunlosky (2013) states, 'Quite often, students believe these relatively ineffective strategies are actually the most effective', and continues to say, 'Unfortunately, in a recent review of the research, my colleagues and I found that these strategies are not that effective.' He adds, 'The good news is that decades of research has focused on evaluating the effectiveness of many promising strategies for helping students learn.' We now need to shift this focus and attention from ineffective strategies to students using effective strategies independently.

Although all aspects of formative assessment lead up to activating learners as owners of their own learning, it does not have to be something that is carried out towards the end of a task, unit or topic. Learners can take responsibility and ownership of their learning at three stages: planning, monitoring and evaluating.

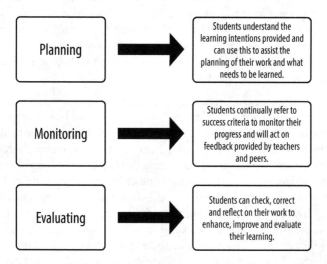

Wiliam and Leahy (2015, p. 169) write that 'learning how to learn' used to be an optional extra in education – today, it's a survival skill. Sherrington (2019b) writes, '"Owning your own learning" is at the heart of strong self-regulation and metacognition: setting learning goals, planning, monitoring and evaluating success in tasks links to those goals; forming effective schemata that take account of big-picture questions and themes that inform subsequent conscious rehearsal and elaboration.' There is a lot more to this strand of formative assessment than there may initially appear on the surface.

Digital tools for plus, minus, interesting

This well-known activity suggested by Wiliam and Leahy (2015) involves instructing students to identify the following, after completing a task:

One thing you found easy +	One thing you found difficult -	One thing you found interesting

We can collect the students' responses in various ways. This can be done individually or as a class so that students can read each other's responses too. It can be completed on post-it notes, mini whiteboards or on flip chart paper. This task can also be carried out digitally using online tools, recommended below. This is a useful form of self-reflection and assessment but can also provide valuable insight for the teacher too.

Google Jamboard

This is a very simple and straightforward digital tool for the classroom. Jamboard can act as a digital sticky note where students write their responses for plus, minus and interesting, using the 'sticky note' function. There can be separate columns or coloured boxes used for plus, minus and interesting or students can respond to all three on the same box. The Jamboard can be on display for the class to read each other's responses or simply on the teacher screen. As with most online tools, the responses can be saved digitally or deleted.

Mentimeter

If you visit Mentimeter.com you can set up a free teacher account and with each presentation you are able to ask three questions (ideal for this task but you can pay to upgrade for access to more features). Once you have set your questions – the plus, minus, interesting – there will be a code to give to students. They need to go to menti.com and submit the code and the questions/prompts will appear on their screen. They do not input their name, which has pros and cons. The anonymity can help students to be more honest, open and reflective but it can be frustrating for both the teacher and student. The teacher can take a snapshot overview of the class responses but won't know who the individual responses belong to (unless the teacher decides to ask) and the student might want their teacher to know what their response included.

Google Forms/Microsoft Forms

It is likely that your school will have a preference for Google or Microsoft Forms but both have similar features and can be used easily for plus, minus, interesting. There is the option to adapt this using a linear scale, for example, 'On a scale of 1-10, 1 being very easy and 10 being very difficult, how would you rate your level of understanding of the lesson/task/unit?' You could then also ask students to elaborate on this as there are options to provide open-ended answers. Results can be anonymous or can include student names/email addresses. Results can be saved, exported or even printed if you wanted but when I have used Google Forms I have kept it simple setting the three questions with the option to respond with either the option for 'short answer text' or 'paragraph'. You can also select 'required' so that students have to submit a response and can't skip an answer.

Flipgrid

The EEF guidance report suggests, 'Teachers should verbalise their metacognitive thinking ("What do I know about problems like this? What ways of solving them have I used before?") as they approach and work through a task.' This approach to recording and reflecting on plus, minus and interesting is different because it focuses on doing so verbally rather than writing/typing and encourages students to verbalise their metacognitive thinking. Flipgrid is a video discussion tool that enables students to record their work, opinions, discussions and reflections verbally. The teacher can then view them, or the videos can be shared with their peers. There is the option to set a timer, with a minimal amount of time and a maximum amount of time for those students who need encouragement to talk for longer or those who need to be stopped from talking for too long! I know many primary teachers that have used Flipgrid in their classroom in a variety of creative and interesting ways and this is another way to do so.

Self-assessment placemat

Similar to the placemats in the previous chapter, the aim of this is to provide instruction and support for students. Sherrington (2019b) puts it so well when he states that 'if a student knows for themselves what they need to do in order to improve and gains the experience of being able to achieve success through applying effort to these self-determined goals, then they begin a positive upward spiral of confidence building, growth mindset-inducing, self-regulation that fuels even more success.'

This placemat should be used to remind students to carry out the following when it comes to checking their own work in order to build their confidence, motivation and success: read, reflect, check and correct. However, students often need more specific guidance than that so I have provided suggestions on the placemat to ensure students understand what self-checking consists of. This could be a placemat or checklist. This is generic but could be adapted and linked to learning intentions and success criteria. It can have a specific literacy focus or subject-specific but, as with all checklists, there is a danger that this improves the work but not the student.

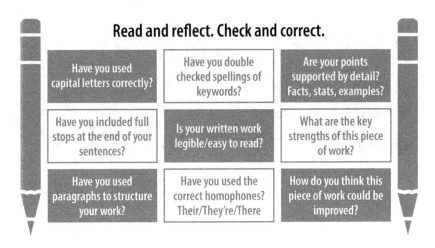

Read and reflect. Check and correct.

Have you used capital letters correctly?	Have you double checked spellings of keywords?	Are your points supported by detail? Facts, stats, examples?
Have you included full stops at the end of your sentences?	Is your written work legible/easy to read?	What are the key strengths of this piece of work?
Have you used paragraphs to structure your work?	Have you used the correct homophones? Their/They're/There	How do you think this piece of work could be improved?

Online self-assessment

More schools are using devices – inside and outside of the classroom – to complete tasks, enhance learning and provide feedback. There are advantages and disadvantages when it comes to technology. There are tools that support teacher workload and allow for creativity and innovation in the classroom that would not be possible without technology, as well as providing flexible approaches to sharing work between the teacher and students. Disadvantages can include the increase of screen time, issues with copying and pasting information and relying on grammar tools to autocorrect spelling and punctuation (this could be argued to be a good or bad thing depending on your viewpoint) that, once again, highlights the distinction between performance and learning. A piece of work may not have any grammatical errors but that doesn't mean students have learned how to use grammar correctly in their written responses.

It is also very likely that our students will use technology either with further/higher education and/or the workplace, therefore being able to confidently and competently communicate online is an important skill.

Based on my experiences of children submitting work online, I created an online learning checklist. This was shared online as a reminder and all students had a copy to refer to. The example shown can be used with different classes and different topics or it can be easily adapted to become more specific. This checklist is to encourage students to become more independent, similar to the example above but with a specific focus on online tasks.

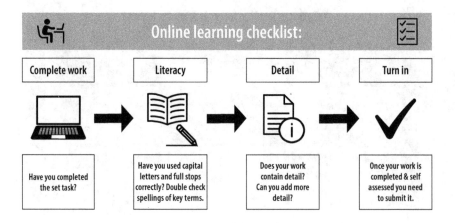

Online learning checklist:			
Complete work	**Literacy**	**Detail**	**Turn in**
Have you completed the set task?	Have you used capital letters and full stops correctly? Double check spellings of key terms.	Does your work contain detail? Can you add more detail?	Once your work is completed & self assessed you need to submit it.

Case study: Self-assessment in action

Jade Pearce is a business studies teacher and Assistant Headteacher responsible for Teaching and Learning at Walton School. Jade and her colleagues have implemented strategies from Wiliam and Leahy's Embedded Formative Assessment *across the curriculum.*

I predominantly use self-assessment when students have completed exam questions. Here, self-assessment ensures that students can assess and, therefore, improve their own writing which enables them to produce work of a higher quality.

To introduce self-assessment successfully, I have found that it is important to make very clear to students what is required, both in terms of the content of the work that students are assessing and how the work should be assessed. This ensures that students are able to self-assess accurately. Firstly, I give clear guidance on the content required for each type of exam question (this is delivered when teaching students how to complete written tasks) and the 'marking' that should be carried out by students when they self-assess their work. For me, in business studies, this includes identifying the answer provided, the number of linked strands of analysis and any application to the specific business/case study.

I, We and You

I then focus on how to assess their work accurately. As with teaching students how to complete any task, this is best done through modelling, guidance and practice. I utilise the I, We, You approach. The following is an example of how I do this.

Firstly, I demonstrate live modelling by assessing a piece of writing 'live'. As I do this, I explain my thought process and why I have awarded certain comments or marks.

We repeat this process as a class, with students making suggestions and explaining their decisions. We also look at examples of work that have already been assessed and discuss why this assessment has been made. Students then work in pairs or small groups to assess work and we discuss this as a class.

Finally, students are asked to assess work independently.

It is important to emphasise that self-assessment is only one way of giving feedback to students and that I will often use it in conjunction with other methods. Before writing, I may use live modelling, deconstruction and paired writing. When students have then completed their independent writing, I may then use live feedback (discussing the work of a number of students, for example through the use of a visualiser) and self-assessment to help students to improve their work.

Self-regulated learning and metacognition with self-testing

I have used self-testing – where students complete questions or activities that require them to recall previous learning – not only to improve students' long-term memories but also their knowledge of their learning through highlighting their areas of strength and gaps in their knowledge. This self-testing is completed both in lessons and for homework. In lessons, I use a range of shorter and less time-consuming activities such as quizzes, keyword retrieval, retrieval grids and 'give me fives' – five facts, five key terms, etc.

I also utilise self-testing in homework. Here, I am able to use longer tasks including those which involve higher-order learning. Examples include retrieval clocks, 'know it all' sheets, 'because, but, so' questions, essay plans and concept maps. In all of these examples, tasks are completed from memory before students gain feedback, either from me or their own study materials. This ensures that students are testing their long-term and not short-term memories and also that they become more aware of what they did or did not know.

I use self-testing to further develop students' metacognition and their ability to assess their own learning accurately by setting tasks that require students to make judgments about their confidence in their learning. For example, this can be achieved by requiring students to put a tick or cross next to each question before they try to complete a quiz. This means students are better able to assess how well they know a topic and, consequently, are more likely to focus on those aspects that their knowledge is weaker in.

Students use self-testing completed in lessons and homework to identify any areas in which they need to conduct further independent study (those aspects or topics that they were unable to recall correctly or fully). To ensure this is completed, I ask students to fill in a simple study log after each self-testing activity to identify the areas or topics they are going to focus on. I then (briefly) check the work that they have produced during this independent study, which may include, for example, flashcards, concept maps or graphic organisers.

This aspect of students owning their own learning depends on them self-testing, and so it is crucial to teach them how to do this effectively. This includes teaching students about short and long-term memory and why techniques such as retrieval practice and interleaving are so effective. It is also crucial to teach students how to use other self-testing methods, such as drawing a concept map or creating flashcards. Modelling this with students in lessons and explaining your thought process, before allowing students to complete guided practice, helps to ensure that students are then able to do this effectively on their own.

You can follow Jade on Twitter @PearceMrs where templates for her resources discussed above can be accessed and downloaded freely.

We need to help our students learn independently but it's easier said than done. Wiliam and Leahy (2015, p. 178) wrote: 'This is very difficult for most teachers because we tend to believe that we are the main causes of student learning. In recent years, study after study shows that the quality of teachers is the most important influence on how much students learn in school. And, on a personal level, we see our students making progress in our lessons, so we believe that we create learning, despite the fact that, deep down, we all know that teachers do not create learning; only learners create learning. What teachers can do is create the circumstances within which learners learn.'

Tips to activate students as owners of their own learning, both inside and outside of the classroom

Provide time	Model self-regulated learning, reflection and assessment
Share examples and exemplars	Provide feedback

- **Provide time:** This should be factored into curriculum design and lesson planning rather than an added five-minute bolt-on when there is an opportunity, opportunities or time don't always arise, hence why we need to plan for them as well as being responsive in the lesson.

- **Model self-regulated learning, reflection and assessment:** This can be done as a live modelling example in class or with scaffolding, such as sentence starters or placemats above that will eventually be removed.

- **Share examples and exemplars:** In the same way that Austin's Butterfly illustrated the power of peer feedback, we can share examples of student work that has significantly improved as a result of self-assessment, reflection and improvement.

- **Provide feedback:** Give students feedback on their self-assessment and improvements so that they are confident in what they are doing and will be able to do so without the teacher, inside or outside of the classroom.

Case study: Formative assessment in action in the primary classroom

All of the strategies in this book have been written about with the aim that they can be applied and adapted across a primary and secondary context. However, as my area of specialism is secondary, I wanted to ensure a wide range of examples and case studies from primary were included too.

Adam Vasco is an experienced primary teacher, Early Years Foundation Stage specialist and former senior leader turned Initial Teacher Trainer. Adam is an advocate for embedding formative assessment strategies in the primary classroom.

Working in Initial Teacher Education (ITE), we use a Netflix analogy: the National Curriculum and Programmes of Study are the series or season. Within each series/season are episodes, these are the learning intentions. Within each episode, the story builds around key points. Here we have the broken-down learning intentions and success criteria. These outcomes run throughout all stages of the lesson.

Every teaching, learning and pedagogical decision is made with these in mind. If we are doing something in the lesson that does not deliver the learning intentions, why are we doing it? These outcomes are free of task and content. As such, any teacher could take these and deliver the learning in very different ways, but the learning outcomes would still be the same, enabling teacher autonomy whilst promoting consistency too.

A good starting point is focusing on the breaking down of the national curriculum and programme of study into SMART (specific, measurable, achievable, relevant and time-bound) learning intentions then strategies to elicit evidence of learning can be put into place. Children should be talking a lot. Talk must be embedded. Learning can be visible. Daily routines that facilitate and make learning visible:

- No hands up, except to ask a question: this can work well in the primary classroom with clear instructions, explanations and focus.
- Think, pair, share: time to think and opportunity to share, but again no hands up, except to ask a question.
- Think aloud: model your own thinking for your students. Do not hide all that internal monologue, let them hear your thought process so that you are modelling and verbalising metacognitive thinking.
- Teacher circulates during talk/group work: listen to the learning!
- Seating plans: a carefully designed seating plan can be used effectively to promote peer support and challenge.
- Whole class activities designed for 'low threshold, high ceiling': these ensure all children can access the task and deepen their understanding as shown in the following example.

'Low threshold, high ceiling': Year 2 subtracting with renaming

Low threshold There are 23 grapes and 5 grapes are eaten. How many grapes are left?

High ceiling Write a note to a friend explaining how they can figure out 23 − 5.

Reflective Which method is better?

Creative Write/draw your own number story which involves subtracting with renaming.

Investigate How many pairs of whole numbers have a difference of 18?

For early years and primary children, it is essential that feedback is simple so that it can be impactful. The vast majority of feedback will be verbal (stamps aren't necessary – we need to ask who the stamps are for). Written feedback must be appropriate to the age of the children and used when the teacher considers it is the most effective and relevant type of feedback for the specific context. It will be the least frequently used form of feedback in most contexts.

Piles. When marking children's work, there are often common themes that occur across all subjects. Rather than be faced with the prospect of writing 30 comments that the children are unlikely to read, create 'piles'. These are common areas for feedback. It could be general or it could be subject-specific. Whatever the common issues are, pile the books together and write a sticky note for that pile which focuses on feedback and, crucially, how this will move learning forward. At the beginning of the next lesson in that subject, address these areas. Ideally, use a visualiser, iPad or tablet to highlight the feedback area. The children can usually spot the mistakes themselves. Children editing their work results in an immediate impact.

Effective peer feedback should be rigorously structured and modelled by the teacher. Children need to be well trained over time to effectively peer assess one another. Scaffolds and models are essential for young children.

A strategy to support this is listening triangles. Children will be allocated three differing roles with increasing levels of difficulty built-in: speaker, listener and responder.

'Listening triangles': Year 1 compose a simple sentence

Using a picture prompt, for example, a jungle image. Mixed prior attainment groupings. Allocate roles based on prior attainment.

Speaker: say a sentence using a subject (name of a place, person or thing) plus a verb to describe what the subject is doing.

Listener: repeat the speaker's sentences. Can you use the conjunction 'and' to join their sentence with one of your own? Remember to use a subject and a verb.

Responder: Write down the sentences both the speaker and the listener said. Can you add an adjective to describe the subject?

> - The ABC strategy (agree, build on, challenge).
> - Display sentence stems for children to use.
>
> Children can – and should – be empowered and provided with the tools to become independent learners. Co-created and shared learning intentions and success criteria, using age-appropriate language, are a must. Practitioners must unpick objectives by asking the children what it is they have to do. This is essential if children are to truly understand what they are striving for and self-assess against when becoming owners of their own learning.
>
> You can follow Adam on Twitter @VascoAdam.

Formative assessment strategies are at the heart of effective teaching and learning. We can continue to use ideas that are tried and tested with the aim of doing the same but better, as we are continually reflecting, learning and improving. There are also new and innovative ways that formative assessment strategies can be applied, both inside and outside of the classroom, for example with the use of many tech tools.

In order for formative assessment strategies to have the desirable and significant impact we hope for, we need to be talking about what and why we are doing what we are doing. These conversations need to occur between teachers at a departmental/phase level, with leaders at all levels and from a whole school perspective. In addition to talking to colleagues, parents and families in the school community should have an awareness and understanding of the strategies so that they too can support and guide their children effectively.

Finally, as stated throughout this book and encouraged by Wiliam and Leahy too, we need to have conversations about formative assessment strategies and techniques with the students in our classrooms. When these conversations become part of the culture and language of learning, students can flourish and become owners of their own learning.

Summary

- Our ultimate goal as teachers is to ensure that our students become confident lifelong learners that continue to flourish once they have left our classroom.

- All of the strands of formative assessment link to this element, we can't rush or skip to this stage.

- Students need to be aware of a range of strategies where they can effectively plan, monitor and evaluate their own learning.

- Motivation and mindset play an important and central role in activating learners as owners of their own learning. This can be achieved through a learning environment that combines support and challenge as well as helpful feedback and genuine praise as a result of student success.

- There are a range of tried and tested techniques that can be used in the classroom to support students with self-reflection and assessment. These can also be done verbally and using a range of online tools too.

REFERENCES

Ball, R. (2020) 'Teach to the Top', *The Educational Imposters* [Blog] 4 July. Retrieved from: www.bit.ly/3xtoINO

Bjork, R. A. and Bjork, E. L. (1992) 'A new theory of disuse and an old theory of stimulus fluctuation'. In A. F. Healy, S. M. Kosslyn, & R. M. Shiffrin (Eds.), *Essays in honor of William K. Estes, Vol. 1. From learning theory to connectionist theory; Vol. 2. From learning processes to cognitive processes* (pp. 35-67). Lawrence Erlbaum Associates, Inc.

Bjork, E. L. and Bjork, R. A. (2011) 'Making things hard on yourself, but in a good way: Creating desirable difficulties to enhance learning'. In M. A. Gernsbacher, R. W. Pew, L. M. Hough, J. R. Pomerantz (Eds.) & FABBS Foundation (Eds.), *Psychology and the real world: Essays illustrating fundamental contributions to society* (pp. 56-64). Worth Publishers.

Black, P. and Wiliam, D. (1998) 'Assessment and Classroom Learning', *Assessment in Education*, 5(1), pp. 7-74.

Black, P. and Wiliam, D. (2009) 'Developing the theory of formative assessment', *Educational Assessment, Evaluation and Accountability*, 21(1), pp. 5-31.

Bloom, B. S., Madaus, G. F. and Hastings, J. T. (1971) *Handbook on Formative and Summative Evaluation of Student Learning*. New York: McGraw-Hill.

Brown, A. L. and Campione, J. C. (1996) 'School for Thought: Overview of the Project and Lessons Learned from One of the Sites'. In L. Schauble and R. Glaser (Eds.), *Innovations in Learning: New Environments for Education*. Abingdon, Oxford: Routledge.

Brown, C. P., Roediger, H. L. and Mcdaniel, M. A. (2014) *Make It Stick: The Science of Successful Learning*. Cambridge, MA: Harvard University Press.

Chandler, P. and Sweller, J. (1991) 'Cognitive Load Theory and the Format of Instruction', *Cognition and Instruction*, 8(4), pp. 293-332.

Chiles, M. (2021) *The Feedback Pendulum*. Melton, Woodbridge: John Catt Educational.

Clarke, S. (2009) 'Learning objectives and success criteria', *Shirley Clarke* [Website]. Retrieved from: www.bit.ly/3hnPuBy

Dunlosky, J. (2013) 'Strengthening the Student Toolbox: Study Strategies to Boost Learning', American Educator [Fall]. Retrieved from: www.bit. ly/3xINmdi

Dylan Wiliam (21 April 2020) *Eliciting evidence of learning.* [Video] YouTube. Retrieved from: www.bit.ly/36jgvzF

Education Endowment Foundation (2018a) 'Feedback', *Teaching and Learning Toolkit.* Retrieved from: www.bit.ly/3k7i24b

Education Endowment Foundation (2018b) 'Metacognition and self-regulation', *Teaching and Learning Toolkit.* Retrieved from: www.bit.ly/3koTS54

Education Endowment Foundation (2018c) 'Peer Tutoring', *Teaching and Learning Toolkit.* Retrieved from: www.bit.ly/3wyQx6d

Education Endowment Foundation (2019) 'Summary of recommendations', *Teaching and Learning Toolkit.* Retrieved from: www.bit.ly/3wLiFTA

EL Education (4 October 2016) *Austin's Butterfly: Models, Critique, and Descriptive Feedback.* [Video] YouTube. Retrieved from: www.bit.ly/3yAZYmQ

Elder, Z. (2012) 'Constructing learning SO THAT it is meaningful and purposeful', *Full On Learning* [Blog] 1 October. Retrieved from: www.bit. ly/3ACG0Ko

Hendrick, C. (2017) 'Five Things I Wish I Knew When I Started Teaching', *chronotope* [Blog] 6 May. Retrieved from: www.bit.ly/3xGSdf1

Hendrick, C. and Macpherson, R. (2017) *What Does This Look Like in The Classroom? Bridging the Gap Between Research and Practice.* Melton, Woodbridge: John Catt Educational.

Learning Sciences International (17 September 20018) *Strategy 1: Clarifying, Sharing, and Understanding Learning Intentions.* [Video] YouTube. Retrieved from: www.bit.ly/3hMghXa

Lori Loehr (26 February 2015) *John Hattie Learning Intentions and Success Criteria.* [Video] YouTube. Retrieved from: www.bit.ly/3hmcIYT

Nuthall, G. (2007) *The Hidden Lives of Learners.* Wellington, New Zealand: NZCER Press.

Pinkett, M. (2017) 'Learning Objectives: a waste of time.', *All Ears* [Blog] 18 April. Retrieved from: www.bit.ly/3wsaN9f

Rickards, F., Hattie, J. and Reid, C. (2021) *The Turning Point for the Teaching Profession*. Abingdon: Routledge.

Sherrington, T. (2017) '#FiveWays of Giving Effective Feedback as Actions', *teacherhead* [Blog] 18 December. Retrieved from: www.bit.ly/3yQIT8D

Sherrington, T. (2019a) '10 Techniques for Retrieval Practice', *teacherhead* [Blog] 3 March. Retrieved from: www.bit.ly/3yJUnef

Sherrington T. (2019b) 'Revisiting Dylan Wiliam's Five Brilliant Formative Assessment Strategies.', *teacherhead* [Blog] 10 January. Retrieved from: www.bit.ly/3hFUkuk

Shute, V. J. (2007) *Focus on Formative Feedback*. ETS. Retrieved from: www.bit.ly/2T6zWJ8

Smith, M. and Weinstein, M. (2016) 'Learn How to Study Using... Elaboration', *The Learning Scientists* [Website] 7 July. Retrieved from: www.bit.ly/3yChmI0

Wiliam, D. and Leahy, S. (2015) *Embedding Formative Assessment: Practical Techniques for K-12 Classrooms*. West Palm Beach, FL: Learning Sciences International.

Wiliam, D. (2020) 'Learning and memory'. In D. Lock (Ed), *The researchEd Guide to Leadership*, pp. 185-197. Melton, Woodbridge: John Catt Educational.

Wiliam, D. and Black, P. J. (1996) 'Meanings and consequences: A basis for distinguishing formative and summative functions of assessment?', *British Educational Research Journal*, 22(5), pp. 537-548.

Wiliam, D. and Black, P. J. (2009) 'Developing the theory of formative assessment', *Educational Assessment, Evaluation, and Accountability*, 21(1), pp. 5-31.

CPSIA information can be obtained
at www.ICGtesting.com
Printed in the USA
JSHW040236170622
27046JS00006B/14